The Quant Trader's Handbook

A COMPLETE GUIDE TO ALGORITHMIC TRADING STRATEGIES AND TECHNIQUES

**WRITTEN BY
JOSH LUBERISSE**

II

THE QUANT TRADER'S HANDBOOK

A Complete Guide to Algorithmic
Trading Strategies and Techniques

Josh Luberisse

Fortis Novum Mundum

Copyright © 2023 Fortis Novum Mundum

All rights reserved

No part of this book may be reproduced, or stored in a retrieval system, or transmitted in any form or by any means, electronic, mechanical, photocopying, recording, or otherwise, without express written permission of the publisher.

Any content provided herein should not be relied upon as advice or construed as providing recommendations of any kind. It is your responsibility to confirm and decide which trades to make. In no event should the content of this correspondence be construed as an express or implied promise or guarantee.

No guarantee of any kind is implied or possible where projections of future conditions are attempted.

None of the content published constitutes a recommendation that any particular security, portfolio of securities, transaction or investment strategy is suitable for any specific person. None of the information providers or their affiliates will advise you personally concerning the nature, potential, value or suitability of any particular security, portfolio of securities, transaction, investment strategy or other matter.

By reading this book, the reader agrees that under no circumstances is the author responsible for any losses, direct or indirect, which are incurred as a result of the use of the information contained within this manuscript, i

Cover design by: Fortis Novum Mundum

DISCLOSURE

This communication is for informational purposes only, and contains general information only. The author, Fortis Novum Mundum, LLC. and Other People's Capital, LLC. are not, by means of this communication, rendering accounting, business, financial, investment, legal, tax, or other professional advice or services. This publication is not a substitute for such professional advice or services nor should it be used as a basis for any decision or action that may affect your business or interests. Before making any decision or taking any action that may affect your business or interests, you should consult a qualified professional advisor. This communication is not intended as a recommendation, offer or solicitation for the purchase or sale of any security. The author, Fortis Novum Mundum, LLC. and Other People's Capital, LLC. do not assume any liability for reliance on the information provided herein.

DISCLAIMER

Any content provided herein should not be relied upon as advice or construed as providing recommendations of any kind. It is your responsibility to confirm and decide which trades to make.

Trade only with risk capital; that is, trade with money that, if lost, will not adversely impact your lifestyle and your ability to meet your financial obligations.

Past results are no indication of future performance.

In no event should the content of this correspondence be construed as an express or implied promise or guarantee.

Trading carries a high level of risk, and may not be suitable for all investors. Before deciding to invest you should carefully consider your investment objectives, level of experience, and risk appetite. The possibility exists that you could sustain a loss of some or all of your initial investment and therefore you should not invest money that you cannot afford to lose. Futures, stocks and options trading involves substantial risk of loss and is not suitable for every investor. The valuation of futures, stocks and options may fluctuate, and, as a result, clients may lose more than their original investment.

The impact of seasonal and geopolitical events is already factored into market prices. The highly leveraged nature of futures trading means that small market movements will have a great impact on your trading account and this can work against you, leading to large losses or can work for you, leading to large gains.

The author of this book is not responsible for any losses incurred as a result of using any of our trading strategies.

Loss-limiting strategies such as stop loss orders may not be effective because market conditions or technological issues may make it impossible to execute such orders. Likewise, strategies using combinations of options and/or futures positions such as "spread" or "straddle" trades may be just as risky as simple long and short positions. Information provided in this correspondence is intended solely for informational purposes and is obtained from sources believed to be reliable. Information is in no way guaranteed.

No guarantee of any kind is implied or possible where projections of future conditions are attempted.

None of the content published constitutes a recommendation that any particular security, portfolio of securities, transaction or investment strategy is suitable for any specific person. None of the information providers or their affiliates will advise you personally concerning the nature, potential, value or suitability of any particular security, portfolio of securities, transaction, investment strategy or other matter.

By reading this book, the reader agrees that under no circumstances is the author responsible for any losses, direct or indirect, which are incurred as a result of the use of the information contained within this manuscript, including but not limited to errors, omissions, or inaccuracies.

"Look at him, that's my quant."

JARED VENNETT, THE BIG SHORT

CONTENTS

Title Page
Copyright
DISCLOSURE
DISCLAIMER
Epigraph
Table of Contents
Preface

DISCLAIMER	1
Chapter 1: Introduction to Algorithmic Trading	3
Chapter 2: Financial Markets Structure, Market Participants and Financial Products	19
Chapter 3: Data Sources and Data Handling	37
Chapter 4: Quantitative Analysis and Modeling	44
Chapter 5: Algorithm Development and Backtesting	65
Chapter 6: Execution and Order Management	77
Chapter 7: Infrastructure and Technology	88
Chapter 8: Regulatory and Compliance Considerations	96
Chapter 9: Building a Successful Algorithmic Trading Business	100
Chapter 10: Advanced Topics in Quantitative Trading	106
Chapter 11: Case Studies and Lessons from Successful	120

Algorithmic Traders	
Conclusion	133
References	137
Acknowledgement	141
About The Author	143
Books In This Series	147
Books By This Author	155

TABLE OF CONTENTS

Preface
    Introduction
    Target Audience
    How to Use This Book

Chapter 1: Introduction to Algorithmic Trading
    a. Definition and overview
    b. Types of algorithmic trading strategies
    c. Advantages and disadvantages

Chapter 2: Financial Markets Structure, Market Participants and Financial Products
    a. Broker-Dealers and Investment Advisers
    b. Securities Exchanges and Alternative Trading Systems
    c. Understanding Financial Instruments

Chapter 3: Data Sources and Data Handling
    a. Types of data (historical, real-time, fundamental, technical, alternative)
    b. Data cleaning and preprocessing
    c. Data storage and management

Chapter 4: Quantitative Analysis and Modeling
    a. Statistical analysis
    b. Time series analysis
    c. Machine learning techniques
    d. Portfolio optimization
    e. Risk management

Chapter 5: Algorithm Development and Backtesting
    a. Defining a trading Hypothesis

      b. Developing a trading Algorithm
      c. Backtesting methodology and considerations
      d. Performance evaluation metrics
      e. Overfitting and model validation

Chapter 6: Execution and Order Management
      a. Order types and execution algorithms
      b. Transaction cost analysis
      c. Managing market impact and Slippage
      d. Liquidity and order routing

Chapter 7: Infrastructure and Technology
      a. Hardware and networking requirements
      b. Software and programming languages
      c. APIs and trading platforms

Chapter 8: Regulatory and Compliance Considerations
      a. Regulatory environment
      b. Best practices for risk management and compliance

Chapter 9: Building a Successful Algorithmic Trading Business
      a. Developing a competitive edge
      b. Intellectual property protection
      c. Team building and talent management
      d. Continuous research and improvement

Chapter 10: Case Studies and Lessons from Successful Algorithmic Traders
      a. Renaissance Technologies and Jim Simons
      b. DE Shaw and David E. Shaw
      c. Two Sigma and Citadel
      d. Other notable quantitative hedge funds and traders

References
   Books, Articles and Websites
   Reports and Studies.

PREFACE

In the rapidly evolving landscape of financial markets, the emergence of algorithmic trading has transformed the way we understand and engage with financial instruments. "The Quant Trader's Handbook" is a comprehensive guide crafted to demystify the complex world of quantitative trading, offering insights into the strategies, technologies, and practices that shape today's financial markets.

This book is the culmination of years of research, practical experience, and collaboration with industry experts. It aims to bridge the gap between academic theory and real-world trading practices, providing readers with a solid foundation in algorithmic trading and a clear understanding of how quantitative strategies are developed and implemented.

As we venture into this journey, we acknowledge the rapid advancements in technology and data science that continually reshape the trading landscape. Hence, this book not only delves into traditional algorithmic strategies but also explores the integration of cutting-edge techniques like machine learning and artificial intelligence in trading.

The journey of writing this book has been both challenging and rewarding. We have endeavored to make complex concepts accessible without sacrificing the depth of analysis. This book is not just a technical guide; it's a narrative that weaves together the history, evolution, and future of quantitative trading.

We extend our gratitude to the many professionals in the field whose insights and experiences have enriched this handbook.

Their contributions have been invaluable in providing a real-world perspective to our discussions.

"The Quant Trader's Handbook" is designed for a wide audience, from aspiring quants to seasoned traders, and even curious individuals seeking to understand the dynamics of modern financial markets. Our hope is that this book serves as a valuable resource, guiding you through the intricacies of algorithmic trading and inspiring you to explore the fascinating world of quantitative finance.

As the financial markets continue to evolve, so will the strategies and technologies discussed in this book. We encourage readers to approach this handbook as a starting point, a foundation upon which to build further knowledge and expertise in the field of quantitative trading.

Welcome to the world of quantitative trading, where data, algorithms, and technology intersect to create new opportunities and challenges. Let's embark on this exciting journey together.

Josh Luberisse

DISCLAIMER

Any content provided herein should not be relied upon as advice or construed as providing recommendations of any kind. It is your responsibility to confirm and decide which trades to make.

Trade only with risk capital; that is, trade with money that, if lost, will not adversely impact your lifestyle and your ability to meet your financial obligations.

Past results are no indication of future performance.

In no event should the content of this correspondence be construed as an express or implied promise or guarantee.

Trading carries a high level of risk, and may not be suitable for all investors. Before deciding to invest you should carefully consider your investment objectives, level of experience, and risk appetite. The possibility exists that you could sustain a loss of some or all of your initial investment and therefore you should not invest money that you cannot afford to lose. Futures, stocks and options trading involves substantial risk of loss and is not suitable for every investor. The valuation of futures, stocks and options may fluctuate, and, as a result, clients may lose more than their original investment.

The impact of seasonal and geopolitical events is already factored into market prices. The highly leveraged nature of futures trading means that small market movements will have a great impact on your trading account and this can work against you, leading to large losses or can work for you, leading to large gains.

The author of this book is not responsible for any losses incurred as a result of using any of our trading strategies.

Loss-limiting strategies such as stop loss orders may not be effective because market conditions or technological issues may make it impossible to execute such orders. Likewise, strategies using combinations of options and/or futures positions such as "spread" or "straddle" trades may be just as risky as simple long and short positions. Information provided in this correspondence is intended solely for informational purposes and is obtained from sources believed to be reliable. Information is in no way guaranteed.

No guarantee of any kind is implied or possible where projections of future conditions are attempted.

None of the content published constitutes a recommendation that any particular security, portfolio of securities, transaction or investment strategy is suitable for any specific person. None of the information providers or their affiliates will advise you personally concerning the nature, potential, value or suitability of any particular security, portfolio of securities, transaction, investment strategy or other matter.

By reading this book, the reader agrees that under no circumstances is the author responsible for any losses, direct or indirect, which are incurred as a result of the use of the information contained within this manuscript, including but not limited to errors, omissions, or inaccuracies.

CHAPTER 1: INTRODUCTION TO ALGORITHMIC TRADING

Definition and Overview

Algorithmic Trading

Algorithmic trading, also known as algo trading or automated trading, refers to the use of computer algorithms to automate the process of placing trades. These algorithms are designed to execute trading strategies based on predefined rules or conditions, such as market trends, technical indicators, or specific events. Algorithmic trading can involve a range of strategies, including quant trading and HFT, as well as other strategies like arbitrage, market making, and trend-following. The main advantage of algorithmic trading is the ability to execute trades more quickly and accurately than humans, reducing the potential for human error and emotional decision-making.

Quantitative (Quant) Trading:

Quant trading refers to investment strategies that rely on advanced mathematical models and statistical analysis to identify trading opportunities. Quant traders use various techniques, including data mining, machine learning, and statistical analysis to develop and test trading strategies. The goal is to exploit patterns and relationships in historical data to make informed investment decisions. Quant trading can be executed manually or through automated systems, depending on the complexity of the model and the trader's preference.

High-Frequency Trading (Hft):

High-frequency trading is a subset of algorithmic trading that involves the rapid execution of trades, typically within milliseconds or microseconds. HFT firms use advanced technology, including powerful computers and low-latency network connections, to analyze market data, identify trading opportunities, and execute trades as quickly as possible. The primary goal is to capitalize on small price discrepancies or market inefficiencies that occur in the very short term. HFT firms often employ sophisticated algorithms to execute their strategies and compete with other firms based on speed and efficiency.

Algorithmic trading has gained significant popularity in the past few decades, thanks to advancements in technology, computing power, and the widespread availability of financial data. Today, algorithmic trading is employed by various market participants, including hedge funds, investment banks, proprietary trading firms, and individual traders. It is estimated that a significant percentage of trading volume in global financial markets is now driven by algorithmic trading systems.

Timeline Of The Evolution Of Algorithmic Trading

Below is a general timeline showcasing the evolution of algorithmic trading, starting from its primitive beginnings to the high-tech systems of today. The narrative intertwines technological advancements with the development of financial markets.

1970s: The Pioneering Days
- 1971: The NASDAQ stock market, the world's first electronic stock market, is founded. This is seen by many as the unofficial beginning of electronic trading.
- Late 1970s: The concept of "program trading" for executing large stock trades automatically begins to take form.

1980s: The Age of Computers
- Early 1980s: Computers start playing a significant role in trading, with algorithms primarily used for splitting large orders to avoid market impact.
- 1983: Bloomberg Terminal is introduced, revolutionizing the way financial data is accessed and used.
- 1987: The Black Monday stock market crash occurs. While its relation to algorithmic trading is debated, it's clear that computerized strategies played some part in the market's decline.

1990s: The Rise of Electronic Trading
- 1990s: Electronic Communication Networks (ECNs) come into play, changing the landscape of trading and paving the way for high-frequency trading.
- Late 1990s: FIX (Financial Information eXchange) Protocol emerges as a new electronic communications protocol for

real-time exchange of securities transactions.

2000s: High-Frequency and Algorithmic Expansion
- Early 2000s: The rise of decimalization reduces the size of the bid-ask spread, making high-frequency trading more viable.
- 2007: NYSE Euronext acquires the Algorithmic Trading Management system, marking a significant endorsement of algorithmic trading by mainstream exchanges.
- 2008: The market sees an uptick in algorithmic trading as technology further advances and regulations become more accommodative.
- 2010: The Flash Crash occurs, leading to increased scrutiny of high-frequency traders and calls for additional regulation.

2010s: Refinement and Regulation
- Early 2010s: Algorithmic strategies diversify, moving beyond equities to forex, commodities, and other asset classes.
- 2014: Michael Lewis's "Flash Boys" is published, critiquing high-frequency trading and leading to widespread debate on its role in the markets.
- Late 2010s: Regulatory bodies worldwide begin implementing tighter rules on algorithmic and high-frequency trading.

2020s: AI and Machine Learning Integration
- Early 2020s: Advanced machine learning and artificial intelligence techniques are integrated into trading strategies, with models being trained on vast datasets to predict price movements.
- Ongoing: Ethical considerations surrounding algorithmic trading rise to the forefront, especially as AI continues to play a more significant role.

While the evolution of algorithmic trading has brought many benefits, such as increased liquidity and tighter spreads, it has also raised concerns. As technology continues to shape the world of finance, the future holds new advancements, challenges, and considerations for algorithmic traders.

Advantages Of Algorithmic Trading

There are several advantages to using algorithmic trading systems, some of which include:

- Speed and Efficiency: Algorithmic trading systems can analyze market data and execute trades at a much faster pace than human traders. This enables them to capitalize on short-term market inefficiencies and rapidly changing conditions that might otherwise be missed by manual trading.

- Accuracy and Consistency: Algo trading systems follow a set of predefined rules and conditions, ensuring that trade execution is consistent and less prone to human errors. This can help reduce the likelihood of costly mistakes and improve overall trading performance.

- Reduced Emotional Impact: One of the most significant challenges faced by human traders is managing emotions, such as fear and greed, which can lead to irrational decisions. Algorithmic trading eliminates this issue by automating the trading process and sticking to the predefined rules without being influenced by emotions.

- Risk Management: Algorithmic trading systems can incorporate sophisticated risk management techniques, such as setting stop-loss orders, position sizing, and diversification, to protect the trading capital and minimize losses.

- Cost Savings: Automated trading can help reduce transaction costs by minimizing the bid-ask spread and taking advantage of more favorable execution prices. Additionally, algorithmic trading can reduce labor costs associated with manual trading and market analysis.

Disadvantages Of Algorithmic Trading

Despite its many advantages, there are also some potential drawbacks to algorithmic trading:

- System Errors and Technical Issues: Algorithmic trading systems rely on technology and software, which can be prone to errors, bugs, or hardware failures. These issues can result in unexpected losses or missed trading opportunities.

- Overfitting and Model Risk: Algorithmic trading strategies are typically developed and tested using historical data. However, there is a risk of overfitting, where a strategy performs exceptionally well on historical data but fails to perform as expected in live trading due to changing market conditions or unforeseen events.

- Regulatory and Compliance Challenges: Algorithmic trading is subject to strict regulations and compliance requirements in many jurisdictions. Traders must ensure that their algorithms comply with relevant rules and regulations to avoid potential penalties or sanctions.

- Market Manipulation Concerns: There have been instances of algorithmic trading systems being used for market manipulation, such as spoofing or layering. This has led to increased scrutiny from regulators and a negative perception of algorithmic trading in some circles.

Despite these challenges, algorithmic trading continues to be a popular and effective method of trading in financial markets. As technology and data availability continue to improve, the potential for further advancements in algorithmic trading is vast.

Below is a network diagram showcasing the interactions between different components of a trading system:

- Data Sources: These provide the necessary data to the system, such as market prices or news feeds.
- Strategy Engines: Using the data, they generate trading signals or orders.
- Risk Management Systems: Before any order is sent for execution, it's evaluated to ensure it doesn't breach predefined risk parameters.
- Execution Engines: These components handle the actual placement of orders in the market.

You can also observe the feedback loops from the Execution Engines back to the Strategy Engines and Risk Management Systems. These loops represent scenarios where real-time feedback from the market might require adjustments or reassessments.

Trading System Network Diagram

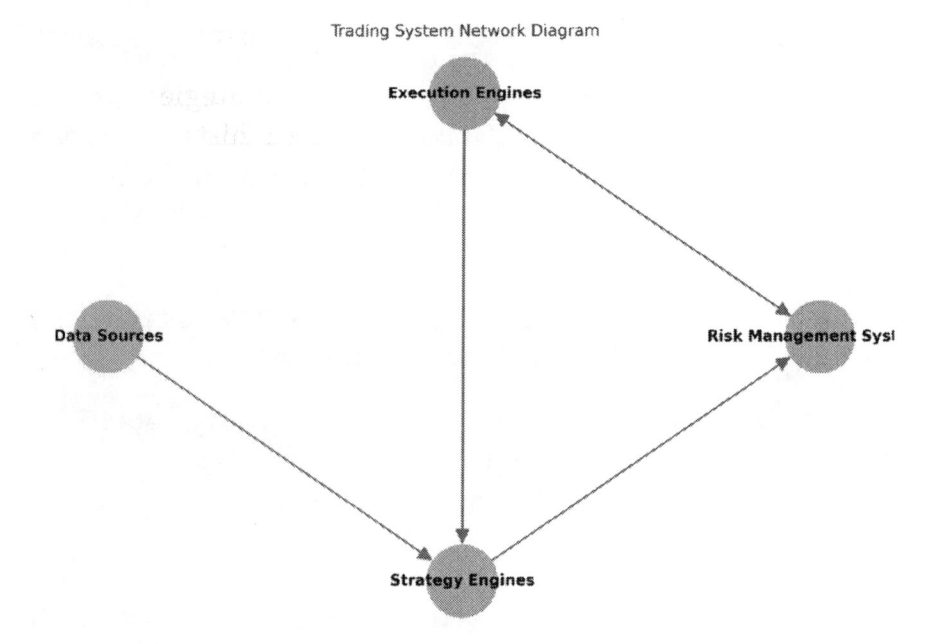

In the upcoming chapters of this book, we will delve deeper into various aspects of algorithmic trading, exploring the strategies, techniques, and tools required to build a successful algorithmic trading system.

Types of Algorithmic Trading Strategies

There is a wide array of algorithmic trading strategies that can be employed to capitalize on different market conditions and trading opportunities. Some of the most common types of algo trading strategies include:

- Momentum and Trend Following: These strategies seek to identify and follow strong price trends or momentum in the market. They typically use technical indicators, such as moving averages, MACD, or RSI, to generate trade signals.

- Mean Reversion: Mean reversion strategies assume that asset prices tend to revert to their historical mean or average levels over time. They aim to capitalize on short-term price deviations from these levels by taking a contrarian position.

- Statistical Arbitrage: Statistical arbitrage strategies involve identifying and exploiting temporary price inefficiencies or mispricings between related financial instruments. These strategies typically rely on sophisticated quantitative models and require high-speed execution to be effective.

- Market Making and Liquidity Provision: Market making strategies involve quoting both buy and sell prices for financial instruments, profiting from the bid-ask spread, and providing liquidity to the market. These strategies require advanced execution algorithms and risk management techniques to manage inventory and limit adverse selection.

- Sentiment Analysis and News-Based Trading: These strategies analyze news data, social media, or other textual data sources to gauge market sentiment and generate trading signals based on the predicted impact of news or sentiment shifts on asset prices.

- High-Frequency Trading (HFT): HFT is a subset of algorithmic trading that involves executing trades at extremely high speeds, often measured in microseconds. HFT strategies seek to capitalize on very short-term price inefficiencies and rely on low-latency infrastructure and advanced execution algorithms.

One of the most popular quantitative trading strategies is the

Moving Average Crossover strategy. It's simple yet effective for many market scenarios. The basic idea is to take two moving averages (typically one short-term and one long-term) and generate buy/sell signals based on how these averages cross over each other.

Below is the pseudocode for a Moving Average Crossover strategy:

```
INITIALIZE account_balance, position = 0
DEFINE short_window = 40   // For a 40-day short-term moving average
DEFINE long_window = 100   // For a 100-day long-term moving average

FOR each trading day as 'day' DO
    Calculate short_moving_average for the past short_window days
    Calculate long_moving_average for the past long_window days

    IF short_moving_average of 'day' > long_moving_average of 'day' AND
        short_moving_average of 'day - 1' <= long_moving_average of 'day - 1' THEN
            IF position <= 0 THEN
                Buy stock to make position = 1
                Deduct purchase amount from account_balance
            END IF

    ELSE IF short_moving_average of 'day' < long_moving_average of 'day' AND
            short_moving_average of 'day - 1' >= long_moving_average of 'day - 1' THEN
            IF position >= 0 THEN
                Sell stock to make position = -1
                Add sale amount to account_balance
            END IF
```

END IF
END FOR

```
INITIALIZE ACCOUNT_BALANCE, POSITION = 0
DEFINE SHORT_WINDOW = 40  // FOR A 40-DAY SHORT-TERM MOVING AVERAGE
DEFINE LONG_WINDOW = 100  // FOR A 100-DAY LONG-TERM MOVING AVERAGE

FOR EACH TRADING DAY AS 'DAY' DO
    CALCULATE SHORT_MOVING_AVERAGE FOR THE PAST SHORT_WINDOW DAYS
    CALCULATE LONG_MOVING_AVERAGE FOR THE PAST LONG_WINDOW DAYS

    IF SHORT_MOVING_AVERAGE OF 'DAY' > LONG_MOVING_AVERAGE OF 'DAY' AND
       SHORT_MOVING_AVERAGE OF 'DAY - 1' <= LONG_MOVING_AVERAGE OF 'DAY - 1' THEN
        IF POSITION <= 0 THEN
            BUY STOCK TO MAKE POSITION = 1
            DEDUCT PURCHASE AMOUNT FROM ACCOUNT_BALANCE
        END IF

    ELSE IF SHORT_MOVING_AVERAGE OF 'DAY' < LONG_MOVING_AVERAGE OF 'DAY' AND
            SHORT_MOVING_AVERAGE OF 'DAY - 1' >= LONG_MOVING_AVERAGE OF 'DAY - 1' THEN
        IF POSITION >= 0 THEN
            SELL STOCK TO MAKE POSITION = -1
            ADD SALE AMOUNT TO ACCOUNT_BALANCE
        END IF

    END IF
END FOR
```

This pseudocode provides a basic implementation of the Moving Average Crossover strategy. In practice, more sophisticated versions might include additional risk management rules, varying the window lengths based on market conditions, or incorporating other indicators.

Remember, while this strategy has proven effective in certain market conditions, no trading strategy guarantees success, and it's important to use them in conjunction with proper risk management techniques.

The author of this book is not responsible for any losses incurred as a result of using any trading strategies. Any content provided herein should not be relied upon as advice or construed as providing recommendations of any kind. It is your responsibility to confirm and decide which trades to make.

Pair Trading Strategy

Pair trading is a market-neutral strategy in which pairs of stocks (typically correlated) are traded in such a way that if one stock in the pair outperforms the other, the outperforming stock is sold short and the underperforming stock is bought.

Here's some pseudocode for a basic Pair Trading strategy:

```
INITIALIZE account_balance
DEFINE threshold = some_value // This is a value beyond which the difference in stock prices is considered significant
DEFINE lookback_period = some_number_of_days

FOR each trading day as 'day' DO
    Calculate the mean difference in price between Stock A and Stock B over the last lookback_period days as 'mean_difference'
    Calculate the standard deviation of the difference in price between Stock A and Stock B over the last lookback_period days as 'std_deviation'
    Calculate the price difference today between Stock A and Stock B as 'current_difference'

    z_score = (current_difference - mean_difference) / std_deviation

    IF z_score > threshold THEN
        // Stock A is significantly overpriced compared to Stock B
```

```
    IF not short on Stock A THEN
        Short Stock A
        Buy Stock B
        Deduct amounts from account_balance
    END IF
  ELSE IF z_score < -threshold THEN
    // Stock B is significantly overpriced compared to Stock A
    IF not short on Stock B THEN
        Short Stock B
        Buy Stock A
        Deduct amounts from account_balance
    END IF
  ELSE
    IF any positions open THEN
        Close all positions
        Update account_balance based on sales
    END IF
  END IF
END FOR
```

```
INITIALIZE account_balance
DEFINE threshold = SOME_VALUE  // This is a value beyond which the difference in stock prices is
considered significant
DEFINE lookback_period = SOME_NUMBER_OF_DAYS

FOR each trading day as 'day' DO
    Calculate the mean difference in price between Stock A and Stock B over the last
lookback_period days as 'mean_difference'
    Calculate the standard deviation of the difference in price between Stock A and Stock B over the
last lookback_period days as 'std_deviation'
    Calculate the price difference today between Stock A and Stock B as 'current_difference'

    z_score = (current_difference - mean_difference) / std_deviation

    IF z_score > threshold THEN
        // Stock A is significantly overpriced compared to Stock B
        IF not short on Stock A THEN
            Short Stock A
            Buy Stock B
            Deduct amounts from account_balance
        END IF
    ELSE IF z_score < -threshold THEN
        // Stock B is significantly overpriced compared to Stock A
        IF not short on Stock B THEN
            Short Stock B
            Buy Stock A
            Deduct amounts from account_balance
        END IF
    ELSE
        IF any positions open THEN
            Close all positions
            Update account_balance based on sales
        END IF
    END IF
END FOR
```

This pseudocode offers a high-level view of the Pair Trading strategy. In real-world applications, it would be essential to consider transaction costs, slippage, capital constraints, and other factors. Furthermore, selection of the stock pairs and the threshold are crucial aspects that would typically involve more sophisticated analysis.

The author of this book is not responsible for any losses incurred as a result of using any trading strategies. Any content provided herein should not be relied upon as advice or construed as providing recommendations of any kind. It is your responsibility to confirm and decide which trades to make.

Getting Started with Algorithmic Trading

Before diving into the world of algorithmic trading, it is essential to understand that success in this field requires a solid foundation in financial markets, programming skills, and quantitative analysis. Here are a few steps to help you get started with algorithmic trading:

- Learn the Basics: Familiarize yourself with the financial markets, trading instruments, and market microstructure. Understand the basic principles of trading, including risk management, position sizing, and trade execution.

- Acquire Programming Skills: Algorithmic trading requires proficiency in programming languages such as Python, C++, or Java. Learn one or more of these languages and become comfortable with using programming libraries and APIs relevant to trading and data analysis.

- Develop Quantitative Skills: Gain a solid understanding of statistics, econometrics, and machine learning techniques, which are essential for developing and testing algorithmic trading strategies.

- Experiment with Trading Strategies: Start by

researching and implementing simple trading strategies based on historical data. Practice backtesting, optimizing, and evaluating the performance of these strategies.

- Continuously Learn and Improve: Algorithmic trading is an evolving field, and it's essential to stay up-to-date with the latest research, techniques, and tools. Attend conferences, read academic papers, and participate in online forums to expand your knowledge and improve your skills.

By following these steps and the guidance provided in this book, you can lay the foundation for a successful algorithmic trading career. In the next chapter, we will explore the different financial markets and instruments that can be traded using algorithmic trading strategies.

CHAPTER 2: FINANCIAL MARKETS STRUCTURE, MARKET PARTICIPANTS AND FINANCIAL PRODUCTS

Financial markets are a complex ecosystem where various participants interact to facilitate the issuance, trading, and management of securities. Understanding the structure of markets, different financial products and the roles of different market participants is essential for anyone pursuing a career as an algorithmic trader. In this chapter, we will provide an overview of the key participants in the securities markets, including broker-dealers, investment advisers, securities exchanges, and alternative trading systems as well as different financial products that are traded including equity securities, debt securities and options.

Broker-Dealers and Investment Advisers

A broker-dealer is a firm or individual engaged in the business of buying and selling securities on behalf of clients (broker) or for their account (dealer). They play a crucial role in facilitating transactions in the securities markets by connecting buyers and sellers. Broker-dealers are subject to various regulations and must register with the SEC and be members of FINRA. There are two main types of broker-dealers:

Full-Service Broker-Dealers

Full-service broker-dealers provide a wide range of services to their clients, including trade execution, investment advice, research, and financial planning. They often charge higher fees or commissions compared to discount broker-dealers but offer more personalized services and support.

Discount Broker-Dealers

Discount broker-dealers focus on providing low-cost trade execution services. They typically offer fewer services compared to full-service broker-dealers and may not provide investment advice or research. Clients of discount broker-dealers often rely on online platforms and tools to manage their investments, and the fees or commissions charged are generally lower.

Investment Advisers

Investment advisers are individuals or firms that provide professional advice on the purchase and sale of securities, as well as other investment-related services, such as portfolio management and financial planning. They are compensated for their advice and typically charge fees based on assets under management (AUM), hourly rates, or fixed fees.

Investment advisers are required to register with the SEC or state securities regulators, depending on the amount of assets they manage. They have a fiduciary duty to act in the best interests of their clients and must disclose any conflicts of interest.

Securities Exchanges and Alternative Trading Systems

Securities Exchanges

Securities exchanges are marketplaces where securities are bought and sold. They provide a platform for investors and traders to transact in a transparent, regulated environment. In the United States, some of the most well-known securities exchanges include the New York Stock Exchange (NYSE), the Nasdaq Stock Market, and the Chicago Board Options Exchange (CBOE).

Securities exchanges have specific listing requirements for companies that want to issue securities and be publicly traded on their platform. These requirements often include financial reporting standards, corporate governance guidelines, and minimum market capitalization thresholds. Exchanges earn revenue from listing fees, transaction fees, and market data fees.

Alternative Trading Systems (ATS)

Alternative Trading Systems (ATS) are private, non-exchange trading venues that facilitate the trading of securities outside of traditional securities exchanges. ATS can include electronic communication networks (ECNs), dark pools, and crossing networks.

Electronic Communication Networks (ECNs)

ECNs are electronic trading systems that automatically match buy and sell orders at specified prices. They provide greater transparency and efficiency by directly connecting buyers and sellers without the need for intermediaries. ECNs charge a fee for each transaction executed on their platform.

Dark Pools

Dark pools are private trading venues that allow participants to execute large block trades without revealing their intentions to the broader market. This lack of transparency can help minimize market impact and protect the participants' trading strategies. However, dark pools have also been criticized for their potential to create a two-tiered market system.

The primary purpose of dark pools is to provide a more discreet environment for large trades that could otherwise impact the market price of a security. When a large order is placed on a public exchange, it can create a significant price movement due to supply and demand dynamics, potentially resulting in a less favorable execution price for the institutional investor. By trading in a dark pool, these large investors can minimize market impact and maintain confidentiality.

Dark pools function as an off-exchange trading venue, matching buy and sell orders without publicly displaying price quotes or order sizes. They typically use electronic communication networks (ECNs) or alternative trading systems (ATS) to facilitate these transactions.

While dark pools offer benefits to institutional investors, they have also faced criticism for their lack of transparency and potential to undermine the price discovery process in public markets. Regulators have been increasingly scrutinizing dark pools to ensure they maintain a fair and orderly trading environment.

Crossing Networks

Crossing networks are ATS that match buy and sell orders at specific times or at specific price levels. They allow for large block trades to be executed with minimal market impact and lower transaction costs. Crossing networks typically cater to institutional investors.

Understanding Financial Products

Equity Securities

Equity securities, also known as stocks or shares, represent ownership interests in a corporation. They provide investors with a claim on a portion of the company's assets and earnings. Equity securities are an essential component of the financial markets and a popular investment vehicle for individual and institutional investors.

This section will cover the main types of equity securities, their characteristics, and the factors that can influence their value.

Types of Equity Securities

There are two primary types of equity securities: common stocks and preferred stocks. Each type has unique features, benefits, and risks associated with them.

Common Stocks

Common stocks are the most prevalent type of equity securities. Owners of common stocks, also known as common shareholders, have voting rights and can participate in the decision-making process of the company, usually through voting at annual general meetings. Common shareholders are entitled to receive dividends, although the payment of dividends is at the discretion of the company's board of directors.

In the event of liquidation, common shareholders have a residual claim on the company's assets after all other obligations, such as debt and preferred stock, have been satisfied.

Preferred Stocks

Preferred stocks are a hybrid form of equity security that combines features of both common stocks and bonds. Preferred shareholders usually do not have voting rights but are entitled to receive dividends before common shareholders. The dividend rate for preferred stocks is typically fixed or can be tied to a benchmark interest rate.

Preferred stocks have a higher claim on the company's assets than common stocks in the event of liquidation. However, they are still subordinate to the company's debt obligations.

Characteristics of Equity Securities

Dividends

Dividends are payments made by a corporation to its shareholders, typically from its earnings. Dividends can be paid in cash, additional shares of stock, or other forms of property. The payment of dividends is not guaranteed, and the company's board of directors determines the amount and frequency of dividend payments.

Capital Appreciation

Capital appreciation is the increase in the value of an equity security over time. Investors can realize capital gains when they sell their shares at a higher price than they initially paid. The potential for capital appreciation is one of the primary reasons investors purchase equity securities.

Voting Rights

Common shareholders have the right to vote on various corporate matters, such as the election of the board of directors, mergers and acquisitions, and changes to the company's bylaws. Voting rights allow shareholders to influence the direction of the company and protect their interests.

Factors Influencing the Value of Equity Securities

Several factors can influence the value of equity securities, including company performance, market conditions, and investor sentiment. Understanding these factors can help investors make informed decisions when buying or selling equity securities.

Company Performance

The financial performance of a company plays a significant role in determining the value of its equity securities. Factors such as revenue growth, profitability, and management effectiveness can impact investor perceptions and influence the demand for the company's shares. Strong financial performance can lead to increased investor confidence and higher share prices, while weak performance can result in declining share prices.

Market Conditions

The overall condition of the financial markets can also influence the value of equity securities. During periods of economic expansion, investor optimism can drive share prices higher, while periods of economic contraction or uncertainty can lead to decreased demand for equities and falling share prices. In addition, market-wide events, such as interest rate changes or regulatory developments, can impact the value of equity securities across various sectors.

Investor Sentiment

Investor sentiment, or market psychology, can also play a role in the valuation of equity securities. Optimism and confidence in the markets can lead to increased demand for equities, while fear and pessimism can result in selling pressure and declining share prices. Investor sentiment can be influenced by factors such as financial news, corporate developments, and broader economic trends.

Industry and Sector Factors

The performance of specific industries or sectors can also impact the value of equity securities. Factors such as technological advancements, changes in consumer preferences, and regulatory shifts can influence the prospects of companies within a particular industry or sector, leading to fluctuations in share prices. Investors should consider the broader trends and dynamics within an industry or sector when analyzing equity securities.

Stock Splits and Reverse Stock Splits

A stock split is a corporate action in which a company increases the number of its outstanding shares by issuing additional shares to existing shareholders. This action typically occurs when a company's share price has risen significantly, making the shares less accessible to small investors. A reverse stock split is the opposite action, in which a company reduces the number of its outstanding shares, effectively increasing the share price. These actions do not change the overall market value of the company but can impact the liquidity and marketability of the shares.

Debt Securities

Debt securities, also known as fixed-income securities or bonds, represent the borrowing of funds by corporations, governments, or other entities. These securities are issued with a promise to repay the principal amount (face value) on a specified date (maturity) and pay interest (coupon) to the bondholder at regular intervals. Debt securities are an essential component of the financial markets and provide investors with an opportunity to earn income and preserve capital.

This section will cover the main types of debt securities, their characteristics, and the factors that can influence their value.

Types of Debt Securities

Debt securities can be classified into several categories based on the issuer, maturity, and other features.

Corporate Bonds

Corporate bonds are debt securities issued by corporations to raise capital for various purposes, such as financing ongoing operations, funding new projects, or refinancing existing debt. Corporate bonds generally offer higher yields compared to government bonds, reflecting the higher risk associated with these securities.

Government Bonds

Government bonds, also known as sovereign bonds, are debt securities issued by national governments to finance public expenditures, such as infrastructure projects or social programs. Government bonds are typically considered lower risk than corporate bonds, as they are backed by the credit and taxing power of the issuing government.

Municipal Bonds

Municipal bonds are debt securities issued by state, county, or local governments, or their agencies, to fund public projects such as roads, schools, and utilities. Municipal bonds can offer tax advantages to investors, as the interest income may be exempt from federal and/or state income taxes.

Characteristics of Debt Securities

Principal and Maturity

Debt securities have a face value, or principal amount, which represents the amount the issuer must repay to the bondholder upon maturity. The maturity date is the date on which the principal amount becomes due and payable. Debt securities can have various maturities, ranging from short-term (less than one year) to long-term (more than ten years).

Interest Payments (Coupon)

Debt securities pay interest, known as the coupon, to the bondholder at regular intervals, typically semi-annually or annually. The coupon rate is expressed as a percentage of the face value and represents the income the bondholder will receive during the life of the bond.

Credit Quality and Ratings

The credit quality of a debt security is an assessment of the issuer's ability to meet its interest and principal repayment obligations. Credit rating agencies, such as Standard & Poor's, Moody's, and Fitch, provide credit ratings that reflect their evaluation of the issuer's creditworthiness. Debt securities with higher credit ratings are considered less risky, while those with lower ratings carry a higher risk of default.

Factors Influencing the Value of Debt Securities

Several factors can influence the value of debt securities, including interest rates, credit quality, and economic conditions. Understanding these factors can help investors make informed decisions when buying or selling debt securities.

Interest Rates

Interest rates have a significant impact on the value of debt securities. When interest rates rise, the prices of existing debt securities generally fall, as newer bonds issued at higher rates become more attractive to investors. Conversely, when interest rates decline, the prices of existing debt securities typically rise, as the fixed interest payments become more attractive compared to the lower rates offered on new bonds.

Credit Quality

Changes in an issuer's credit quality can affect the value of its debt securities. An improvement in credit quality, such as an upgrade in credit rating, can lead to an increase in the value of the issuer's bonds. Conversely, a deterioration in credit quality, such as a downgrade in credit rating or a default, can result in a decrease in the value of the issuer's bonds.

Economic Conditions

Economic conditions can also influence the value of debt securities. During periods of economic growth, the demand for corporate bonds may increase as investors seek higher yields and are more willing to take on risk. In contrast, during periods of economic uncertainty or contraction, investors may prefer the relative safety of government bonds, driving up their prices.

Inflation

Inflation, the rate at which the general level of prices for goods and services is rising, can impact the value of debt securities. Higher inflation can erode the purchasing power of the fixed interest payments, reducing the attractiveness of bonds and potentially leading to lower bond prices.

Risks Associated with Investing in Debt Securities

Investing in debt securities carries risks, and it is essential for investors to be aware of these risks before making investment decisions. Some of the primary risks include:

Interest Rate Risk

Interest rate risk is the potential for losses due to changes in interest rates, which can cause bond prices to fluctuate. Longer-term bonds are generally more sensitive to interest rate changes than shorter-term bonds.

Credit Risk

Credit risk is the risk that the issuer of a debt security will default on its interest or principal repayment obligations. Bonds with lower credit ratings carry a higher risk of default.

Reinvestment Risk

Reinvestment risk is the risk that an investor will be unable to reinvest the proceeds from a maturing bond or interest payments at a comparable rate of return. This risk is more pronounced in a declining interest rate environment.

Inflation Risk

Inflation risk is the risk that the purchasing power of the fixed interest payments from a bond will be eroded over time due to rising inflation. Inflation-protected securities, such as Treasury Inflation-Protected Securities (TIPS), can help mitigate this risk.

Options

Options are financial derivatives that give the buyer the right, but not the obligation, to buy or sell an underlying asset at a specified price, called the strike price, on or before a predetermined expiration date. There are two types of options: call options and put options. This section will cover the basics of options, their characteristics, and how they can be used in various investment strategies.

Types of Options

Call Options

A call option gives the buyer the right, but not the obligation, to purchase an underlying asset, such as a stock, at a specified price (the strike price) on or before a predetermined expiration date. The buyer of a call option pays a premium to the seller, or writer, of the option for this right. If the price of the underlying asset rises above the strike price before the expiration date, the buyer can exercise the option and purchase the asset at the lower strike price, potentially realizing a profit. If the price of the underlying asset does not rise above the strike price, the option expires worthless, and the buyer loses the premium paid.

Put Options

A put option gives the buyer the right, but not the obligation, to sell an underlying asset at a specified price (the strike price) on or before a predetermined expiration date. The buyer of a put option pays a premium to the seller for this right. If the price of the underlying asset falls below the strike price before the expiration date, the buyer can exercise the option and sell the asset at the higher strike price, potentially realizing a profit. If the price of the underlying asset does not fall below the strike price, the option expires worthless, and the buyer loses the premium paid.

Characteristics of Options

Option Premium

The option premium is the price that the buyer pays to the seller for the right to buy or sell the underlying asset. The premium is determined by several factors, including the current price of the underlying asset, the strike price, the time until expiration, the volatility of the underlying asset, and prevailing interest rates. Option premiums are quoted on a per-share basis, and most option contracts represent 100 shares of the underlying asset.

Intrinsic Value and Time Value

The option premium can be divided into two components: intrinsic value and time value.

Intrinsic Value

Intrinsic value represents the difference between the current price of the underlying asset and the strike price, if the option is in-the-money. For call options, intrinsic value is the amount by which the underlying asset's price exceeds the strike price. For put options, intrinsic value is the amount by which the strike price exceeds the underlying asset's price. If the option is out-of-the-money, the intrinsic value is zero.

Time Value

Time value represents the portion of the option premium that is attributable to the time remaining until expiration. Time value is influenced by the volatility of the underlying asset and the time until expiration. As the expiration date approaches, the time value of the option decreases, a phenomenon known as time decay.

Trading and Exercising Options

Trading Options

Options are traded on organized exchanges, such as the Chicago Board Options Exchange (CBOE), through a standardized contract with a specified expiration date and strike price. Investors can buy and sell options through a brokerage account, and the transactions are facilitated by market makers who maintain a liquid market in the options.

Exercising Options

When the holder of an option decides to exercise the option, they can either buy (for call options) or sell (for put options) the underlying asset at the specified strike price. The exercise process can vary depending on the type of option and the specific terms of the contract. There are two primary methods of exercising options: American-style and European-style.

American-style Options

American-style options can be exercised at any time before the expiration date. The holder of an American-style option may choose to exercise the option early if it is advantageous to do so, such as when a call option's intrinsic value exceeds the potential future time value, or when a put option is deep in-the-money.

European-style Options

European-style options can only be exercised on the expiration date. European-style options do not allow for early exercise, which can reduce the risk of early assignment for option sellers.

Option Settlement

When an option is exercised, the transaction must be settled. Settlement can occur in one of two ways: physical settlement or cash settlement.

Physical Settlement

In a physical settlement, the underlying asset is delivered by the option writer to the option buyer. For stock options, this involves the transfer of shares from the writer's account to the buyer's account. Physical settlement is the most common form of settlement for equity options.

Cash Settlement

In a cash settlement, the option writer pays the option buyer the cash difference between the market price of the underlying asset and the strike price, multiplied by the number of shares represented by the option contract. Cash settlement is more common for index options and certain financial derivatives.

Option Trading Strategies

Options can be used in various investment strategies, ranging from conservative to speculative. Some common option strategies include:

Covered Call

A covered call strategy involves holding a long position in an underlying asset, such as a stock, and selling call options on that asset. The strategy generates income from the option premium and can provide a limited hedge against potential declines in the asset's value.

Protective Put

A protective put strategy involves holding a long position in an underlying asset and buying put options on that asset. This strategy provides downside protection, as the put options can be exercised to sell the asset at the strike price if its market value falls below the strike price.

Straddle

A straddle strategy involves buying both a call option and a put option with the same strike price and expiration date. This strategy can profit from significant price movements in the underlying asset, in either direction, as long as the price change is large enough to offset the combined cost of the options.

Vertical Spread

A vertical spread strategy involves buying and selling options of the same type (either calls or puts) with the same expiration date, but with different strike prices. Vertical spreads can be used to generate income, hedge existing positions, or speculate on the direction of an asset's price movement.

Factors Affecting Option Prices

Several factors influence the price of an option, including the underlying asset's price, the option's strike price, the time until expiration, the volatility of the underlying asset, and interest rates. These factors are commonly referred to as the option's "Greeks" and include delta, gamma, theta, vega, and rho.

Delta

Delta measures the sensitivity of an option's price to changes in the price of the underlying asset. For call options, delta is positive, indicating that the option's price increases as the underlying asset's price increases. For put options, delta is negative, indicating that the option's price decreases as the underlying asset's price increases. Delta is expressed as a decimal and typically ranges from 0 to 1 for call options and -1 to 0 for put options.

Gamma

Gamma measures the rate of change of delta with respect to changes in the price of the underlying asset. In other words, gamma indicates how sensitive an option's delta is to changes in the underlying asset's price. Gamma is highest for options that are at-the-money and decreases as options move further in- or out-of-the-money.

Theta

Theta measures the sensitivity of an option's price to the passage of time, or time decay. Theta is negative for both call and put options, indicating that the option's price generally decreases as time passes. Theta is typically highest for at-the-money options and decreases as options move further in- or out-of-the-money.

Vega

Vega measures the sensitivity of an option's price to changes in the volatility of the underlying asset. Vega is positive for both call and put options, indicating that the option's price generally

35

increases as the underlying asset's volatility increases. Vega is typically highest for at-the-money options and decreases as options move further in- or out-of-the-money.

Rho

Rho measures the sensitivity of an option's price to changes in interest rates. Rho is positive for call options and negative for put options, indicating that the option's price generally increases as interest rates increase for call options and decreases for put options. Rho is typically highest for in-the-money options and decreases as options move further out-of-the-money.

CHAPTER 3: DATA SOURCES AND DATA HANDLING

Types of Data (historical, real-time, fundamental, technical, alternative)

Data is the lifeblood of algorithmic trading. Accurate, timely, and relevant data is critical for developing, testing, and executing trading strategies. There are several types of data used in algorithmic trading, which can be broadly categorized as follows:

- Historical Data: Historical data refers to historical prices, volume, and other trading-related information for various financial instruments. This data is essential for backtesting and analyzing trading strategies.

- Real-Time Data: Real-time data refers to live market data, such as prices, volume, and order book information. This data is crucial for executing algorithmic trading strategies in real-time.

- Fundamental Data: Fundamental data includes financial statements, economic indicators, and other macroeconomic data that can be used to analyze the intrinsic value of financial instruments and identify trading opportunities.

- Technical Data: Technical data consists of price-derived indicators, such as moving averages, oscillators, and chart patterns, used in technical analysis to generate trading signals.

- Alternative Data: Alternative data refers to non-traditional data sources, such as social media sentiment, satellite imagery, and web traffic data, which can provide unique insights into market trends and trading opportunities.

Data Sources

There are numerous data sources available for algorithmic traders to access the different types of data required for their strategies. Some popular data sources include:

- Exchanges and Market Data Providers: Most financial exchanges and market data providers offer access to historical and real-time market data, either through their proprietary platforms or via third-party data vendors. Examples include NYSE, Nasdaq, CME, and Bloomberg.

- Data Vendors: Numerous data vendors specialize in providing financial market data, such as historical prices, fundamental data, and alternative data. Examples include Quandl, Intrinio, and FactSet.

- Brokerage APIs: Many brokers offer APIs that provide access to real-time market data and trading functionality. Examples include Interactive Brokers, Alpaca, and OANDA.

- Public Data Sources: Government agencies, central banks, and international organizations often publish economic and financial data that can be used for algorithmic trading. Examples include the U.S. Bureau of Economic Analysis (BEA), the Federal Reserve, and the World Bank.

- Web Scraping: Traders can use web scraping techniques to extract financial data from websites, news articles, and other online sources.

Data Cleaning and Preprocessing

Data quality is paramount in algorithmic trading, as inaccurate or incomplete data can lead to erroneous trading signals and poor performance. Before using financial data in trading strategies, it is essential to clean and preprocess the data to ensure its accuracy and consistency. Common data cleaning and preprocessing tasks include:

- Handling Missing Data: Financial data can sometimes contain missing or incomplete values. Depending on the nature and extent of the missing data, traders can choose to fill the gaps using various techniques, such as interpolation or forward/backward filling, or simply remove the affected data points.

- Data Alignment: When working with multiple data sources or time series, it is important to align the data to a common time frame and frequency. This can involve resampling, aggregating, or interpolating data as needed.

- Dealing with Outliers: Outliers are data points that are significantly different from the rest of the data set. They can be caused by data entry errors, extreme market events, or other factors. Outliers can be detected using various statistical techniques and can be removed or adjusted, depending on the context and the trader's discretion.

- Data Transformation: Data transformation involves converting raw data into a format more suitable for analysis or use in trading algorithms. This can include normalizing or scaling data, calculating returns, applying logarithmic transformations, or creating custom indicators.

Feature engineering is the process of creating new variables or features from raw data to improve the predictive power of a trading algorithm. These features can help capture complex relationships within the data and enhance the performance of machine learning or statistical models used in algorithmic trading strategies. Common feature engineering techniques include:

- Technical Indicators: Calculate technical indicators,

such as moving averages, RSI, or MACD, to capture market trends and momentum.

- Ratios and Derived Metrics: Create new variables by combining existing data points, such as price-to-earnings (P/E) ratio or return on equity (ROE), to measure the relative value or performance of financial instruments.

- Interactions and Polynomial Terms: Generate interaction terms between variables or create polynomial terms to capture non-linear relationships in the data.

- Time-Based Features: Create time-based features, such as day of the week, month, or seasonality patterns, to capture time-dependent trends in the data.

- Textual Features: Extract features from textual data, such as news headlines or financial statements, using natural language processing (NLP) techniques to analyze sentiment, word frequency, or topic modeling.

Data Storage and Management

Efficient data storage and management are crucial for algorithmic trading, as traders often work with large volumes of data from various sources. Proper data storage and management practices can help ensure data integrity, improve performance, and facilitate collaboration among team members. Some popular data storage and management solutions for algorithmic trading include:

- Relational Databases: Relational databases, such as MySQL, PostgreSQL, or Microsoft SQL Server, are widely used for storing and managing structured financial data. They provide robust querying capabilities and can handle large volumes of data.

- Time Series Databases: Time series databases, such as InfluxDB or TimescaleDB, are designed specifically for handling time series data and can offer better performance and scalability for time-stamped financial data.

- Flat Files: Flat files, such as CSV or Excel files, can be used for storing smaller data sets or for sharing data with team members. They can be easily read and written using various programming languages and libraries.

- Cloud Storage: Cloud storage services, such as Amazon S3, Google Cloud Storage, or Microsoft Azure Blob Storage, can be used for storing and managing large volumes of data. They offer scalability, redundancy, and easy access from anywhere with an internet connection.

Data Security and Compliance

Data security and compliance are critical aspects of data handling in algorithmic trading, as traders often work with sensitive financial data and personal information. It is essential to follow best practices for data security and adhere to relevant regulations and industry standards, such as the General Data Protection Regulation (GDPR) or the Payment Card Industry Data Security Standard (PCI DSS). Some common data security and compliance practices include:

- Data Encryption: Encrypt data both at rest and in transit using strong encryption algorithms and secure key management practices.

- Access Controls: Implement access controls and authentication mechanisms to restrict access to sensitive data and trading systems.

- Data Backup and Recovery: Regularly back up data and ensure that a robust data recovery plan is in place in case of data loss or system failure.

- Security Monitoring and Auditing: Monitor and audit data access, system activity, and security events to detect and respond to potential security threats or breaches.

- Compliance Policies and Procedures: Establish and maintain data handling policies and procedures that comply with relevant regulations and industry standards.

CHAPTER 4: QUANTITATIVE ANALYSIS AND MODELING

Quantitative analysis is the application of mathematical and statistical techniques to analyze financial markets and develop trading strategies. It involves the use of quantitative models, algorithms, and data-driven insights to identify patterns and relationships in market data and make informed trading decisions. Quantitative analysis forms the backbone of algorithmic trading and is critical for developing, testing, and executing systematic trading strategies.

In this chapter, we will discuss the key concepts, techniques, and tools used in quantitative analysis for algorithmic trading, including:

- Statistical Analysis
- Time Series Analysis
- Econometric Models
- Machine Learning and Artificial Intelligence
- Risk Management and Portfolio Optimization
- Performance Measurement and Evaluation

Statistical Analysis

Statistical analysis is the foundation of quantitative trading and involves using various statistical techniques to summarize, describe, and analyze financial data. Some of the most common statistical methods used in algorithmic trading include:

- Descriptive Statistics: Descriptive statistics summarize and describe the main features of a data set, including measures of central tendency (mean, median, mode), dispersion (range, variance, standard deviation), and shape (skewness, kurtosis). These statistics can help traders understand the distribution and characteristics of their data and inform their trading decisions.

- Inferential Statistics: Inferential statistics use data samples to make inferences about the larger population or underlying data-generating process. This can involve techniques such as hypothesis testing, confidence intervals, and correlation analysis, which can help traders identify statistically significant relationships, trends, or patterns in the data.

- Regression Analysis: Regression analysis is a statistical technique used to model the relationship between a dependent variable (e.g., asset returns) and one or more independent variables (e.g., market factors, technical indicators). Linear regression, logistic regression, and multiple regression are common types of regression analysis used in algorithmic trading to predict asset prices or returns, identify risk factors, and develop trading signals.

Time Series Analysis

Time series analysis is a specialized branch of statistics focused on analyzing and modeling time-ordered data, such as asset prices, returns, or trading volumes. Time series analysis techniques can help traders identify and exploit temporal patterns, trends, and dependencies in financial data. Some key time series analysis methods used in algorithmic trading include:

- Autocorrelation and Partial Autocorrelation: Autocorrelation measures the degree of similarity between a time series and a lagged version of itself, while partial autocorrelation measures the correlation between a time series and its lagged values after removing the effect of any intermediate lags. These measures can help traders identify and model the temporal dependencies in their data.

- Stationarity and Unit Root Tests: Stationarity is an important property of time series data that affects the behavior and forecasting performance of time series models. Stationary time series have a constant mean, variance, and autocorrelation structure over time, while non-stationary time series exhibit trends, seasonality, or other time-varying patterns. Unit root tests, such as the Augmented Dickey-Fuller (ADF) or Phillips-Perron (PP) tests, can be used to test for stationarity and inform the choice of time series models.

- Autoregressive (AR), Moving Average (MA), and ARIMA Models: Autoregressive (AR) models express the current value of a time series as a linear combination of its past values, while moving average (MA) models express the current value as a linear combination of past error terms. Autoregressive integrated moving average (ARIMA) models combine the AR and MA components and can also account for non-stationarity through differencing. These models can be used to forecast asset prices or returns and develop trading signals in algorithmic trading strategies.

- Seasonal Decomposition and Exponential Smoothing: Seasonal decomposition techniques, such as the classical decomposition or STL decomposition, can be used to decompose a time series into its trend, seasonal, and residual components. Exponential smoothing methods, such as Simple Exponential Smoothing (SES), Holt's Linear Trend Model, and Holt-Winters Seasonal Model, are used to forecast time series data with trends and seasonality by applying weighted averages of past observations.

- GARCH and Volatility Models: Generalized Autoregressive Conditional Heteroskedasticity (GARCH) models are used to model and forecast the volatility of financial time series. These models capture the clustering and persistence of volatility observed in financial markets and can be used to estimate risk measures, such as Value-at-Risk (VaR) or Conditional Value-at-Risk (CVaR), and develop volatility-based trading strategies.

Econometric Models

Econometric models are statistical models used to analyze the relationships between economic variables, such as asset prices, interest rates, inflation, and GDP. These models can help traders understand the drivers of asset prices and macroeconomic trends and develop trading strategies based on economic factors. Some common econometric models used in algorithmic trading include:

- Vector Autoregression (VAR) and Vector Error Correction Models (VECM): VAR models are multivariate time series models that capture the interdependencies between multiple time series variables. VECM models extend VAR models to account for cointegration relationships between non-stationary time series. These models can be used to analyze and forecast the joint behavior of multiple financial assets, such as stock indices, currencies, or commodities, and develop pairs trading or arbitrage strategies.

- Cointegration and Pairs Trading: Cointegration is a statistical relationship between two or more non-stationary time series that share a common stochastic trend. Pairs trading is a market-neutral trading strategy that exploits cointegration relationships between financial assets by taking long and short positions in the assets to profit from their mean-reverting behavior. Cointegration tests, such as the Engle-Granger or Johansen tests, can be used to identify cointegrated asset pairs and inform pairs trading strategies.

- Factor Models: Factor models are used to decompose asset returns into a set of underlying factors that drive their behavior. These factors can include market-wide factors, such as market returns or interest rates, industry-specific factors, such as sector returns or commodity prices, or firm-specific factors, such as earnings or dividend yields. Factor models can help traders identify the sources of risk and return in their portfolios and develop factor-based trading strategies.

Machine Learning And Artificial Intelligence

Machine learning and artificial intelligence (AI) techniques have become increasingly popular in algorithmic trading due to their ability to learn complex patterns and relationships in financial data and adapt to changing market conditions. Some common machine learning and AI techniques used in algorithmic trading include:

- Supervised Learning: Supervised learning algorithms, such as linear regression, support vector machines (SVM), or neural networks, learn a mapping between input features (e.g., technical indicators, macroeconomic data) and a target output (e.g., asset returns, price direction) based on a set of labeled training data. These algorithms can be used to develop predictive trading models and generate trading signals.

- Unsupervised Learning: Unsupervised learning algorithms, such as clustering or dimensionality reduction techniques, learn the structure and relationships within the data without the need for labeled training data. These algorithms can be used to discover hidden patterns or groupings in financial data, such as market regimes, asset clusters, or trading styles.

- Reinforcement Learning: Reinforcement learning algorithms learn to make decisions by interacting with an environment and receiving feedback in the form of rewards or penalties. These algorithms can be used to develop adaptive trading strategies that learn and optimize their actions over time based on market feedback. Examples of reinforcement learning techniques used in algorithmic trading include Q-learning, Deep Q-Networks (DQN), and Proximal Policy Optimization (PPO).

- Natural Language Processing (NLP): NLP techniques are used to analyze and extract information from textual data, such as news articles, financial reports, or social media posts. Sentiment analysis, topic modeling, and named entity recognition are some common NLP tasks that can help traders incorporate qualitative information into their quantitative trading models and generate trading signals based on news or market sentiment.

Machine Learning in Market Prediction

The integration of machine learning (ML) in financial markets has opened new frontiers in market prediction. This section introduces the fundamental concepts of ML and their relevance in financial analysis, emphasizing the shift from traditional statistical methods to more sophisticated, data-driven approaches.

Key Machine Learning Techniques for Market Prediction

Linear Regression Models

Linear regression models are foundational in predicting financial market trends. Simple linear regression can predict an asset's future price by establishing a linear relationship between time and price. Multiple regression extends this by incorporating numerous independent variables, such as economic indicators or other asset prices, to enhance the prediction accuracy. These models are especially useful for capturing the trend over time and are straightforward to implement, which makes them a good starting point for quantitative analysis in trading.

Classification Algorithms

Classification algorithms are crucial for categorizing data into predefined classes. In finance, logistic regression can predict binary outcomes like price increase or decrease, while decision trees can map out the decision-making process for buying or selling assets. Random forests, an ensemble of decision trees, improve prediction robustness by reducing variance. These models can help in constructing trading signals when the outcome is categorical.

Support Vector Machines (SVMs)

Support Vector Machines (SVMs) are versatile in handling both classification and regression tasks. In the context of financial markets, SVMs can be employed to discern complex patterns and make predictions about future market behavior. Their ability to handle high-dimensional data and identify optimal separating hyperplanes makes them particularly effective for financial applications where the decision boundary is not readily apparent.

Neural Networks

Neural Networks, particularly feedforward and recurrent neural networks (RNNs), offer powerful tools for financial predictions. Feedforward neural networks can approximate any function, capturing the non-linear relationships in market data. RNNs, which are adept at processing sequential data, can take into account the temporal dynamics of stock prices, making them suitable for time series forecasting. Their adaptability and capacity for learning complex patterns enable them to outperform traditional models in many cases.

Feature Selection and Data Preprocessing

Feature selection is a critical process in preparing data for machine learning models in market prediction. It involves identifying the most relevant variables that contribute to the predictive power of the model, thus enhancing efficiency and accuracy. Techniques such as backward elimination, forward selection, and regularisation methods like Lasso are used for selecting pertinent features and reducing dimensionality. This step not only streamlines the model but also helps in avoiding the curse of dimensionality which can lead to overfitting.

Data cleaning and preprocessing are fundamental to machine learning in finance. It encompasses dealing with missing values, outliers, and errors that could skew the model's performance. Normalization, such as Min-Max scaling, and transformation, such as log transformation, are applied to ensure that the model receives high-quality input data. Properly preprocessed data can significantly impact the reliability of market predictions.

Model Training and Validation

Training ML models is a delicate balance between fitting the data well and maintaining the model's ability to generalize to new, unseen data. Selection of appropriate training datasets is crucial, as is the use of techniques like k-fold cross-validation to prevent overfitting. Regularization techniques such as Ridge and Lasso can also be employed to maintain model simplicity and robustness.

Cross-validation and model testing are not just steps but philosophies ingrained in the model development process. They are about continuously challenging the model with new data, evaluating its performance, and refining its predictive abilities.

Overfitting remains a perennial challenge in financial modeling, more so due to market noise which can lead to deceptive patterns. Techniques like cross-validation, regularization, and ensemble methods are crucial in mitigating these risks.

Market dynamics and non-stationarity pose a unique challenge to ML models in finance. Models must be adaptive and frequently updated to remain relevant as financial markets are influenced by myriad factors that evolve over time. Techniques like rolling windows and expanding windows for model training and validation can help address non-stationarity.

Each of these areas contributes to the robustness and effectiveness of ML models in market prediction, and a nuanced understanding of them is vital for any quant trader looking to leverage machine learning for trading strategies.

Risk Management And Portfolio Optimization

Risk management and portfolio optimization are essential components of quantitative trading that focus on managing the risks and performance of a trading portfolio. These techniques can help traders achieve a balance between risk and return, diversify their investments, and maximize their risk-adjusted performance. Some key risk management and portfolio optimization concepts and methods include:

- Portfolio Theory and Diversification: Portfolio theory, as introduced by Harry Markowitz, provides a framework for constructing efficient portfolios that maximize expected return for a given level of risk or minimize risk for a given level of expected return. Diversification is the process of combining multiple assets with different risk-return characteristics to reduce the overall risk of a portfolio. The concept of correlation between assets plays a critical role in portfolio diversification.

- Modern Portfolio Theory (MPT): MPT is an extension of portfolio theory that incorporates additional assumptions and techniques, such as the Capital Asset Pricing Model (CAPM), the Black-Litterman model, or the Fama-French factor model. These models can help traders estimate the expected return and risk of financial assets, construct optimal portfolios, and evaluate the performance of their trading strategies.

- Risk Measures and Metrics: Risk measures and metrics quantify the potential loss or uncertainty associated with a financial asset or portfolio. Some common risk measures used in algorithmic trading include standard deviation, beta, Value-at-Risk (VaR), Conditional Value-at-Risk (CVaR), and maximum drawdown. These measures can help traders assess and manage the risks of their trading strategies and make informed portfolio allocation decisions.

- Portfolio Optimization Techniques: Portfolio optimization techniques are used to select the optimal weights or allocations of financial assets in a portfolio. These techniques can include mean-variance optimization, which minimizes portfolio variance subject to a target return or maximizes portfolio return subject to a target variance, or more advanced methods, such as robust optimization, Bayesian optimization, or multi-objective optimization.

Performance Measurement And Evaluation

Performance measurement and evaluation are important aspects of quantitative trading that help traders assess the effectiveness and profitability of their trading strategies. Some common performance measurement and evaluation techniques used in algorithmic trading include:

- Performance Metrics: Performance metrics are used to quantify the return, risk, or risk-adjusted performance of a trading strategy or portfolio. Examples of performance metrics include total return, annualized return, Sharpe ratio, Sortino ratio, Calmar ratio, and information ratio.

- Benchmarking and Performance Attribution: Benchmarking involves comparing the performance of a trading strategy or portfolio to a reference index or benchmark, such as the S&P 500, to evaluate its relative performance. Performance attribution is the process of decomposing a strategy's performance into various sources, such as asset allocation, security selection, or market timing, to identify the factors driving its performance.

- Backtesting and Out-of-Sample Testing: Backtesting is the process of simulating the historical performance of a trading strategy using historical data to assess its profitability, risk, and robustness. Out-of-sample testing involves evaluating a strategy's performance on a separate set of data that was not used in the strategy development process to validate its performance and avoid overfitting. Both backtesting and out-of-sample testing are crucial steps in the development and evaluation of algorithmic trading strategies.

- Cross-Validation and Model Selection: Cross-validation is a statistical technique used to assess the performance and generalizability of a predictive model by partitioning the data into multiple training and validation sets. Model selection involves choosing the best model or set of parameters for a trading strategy based on its cross-validated performance. These techniques can help traders avoid overfitting and improve the robustness of their trading models.

- Performance Monitoring and Strategy Adjustment: Performance monitoring involves tracking the real-time performance of a trading strategy or portfolio and comparing it to its historical or expected performance. Strategy adjustment is the process of modifying or updating a trading strategy based on its performance or changing market conditions. Regular performance monitoring and strategy adjustment can help traders maintain the effectiveness and profitability of their algorithmic trading strategies.

Portfolio optimization

The true essence of a successful algorithmic trading system is not simply about identifying winning trades; it's about constructing an optimal portfolio that can weather the storms of the market and deliver consistent performance over time. Portfolio optimization is a multi-faceted process that balances the potential for profit with the need for risk management, and it is a critical element in the toolbox of any quant trader.

Portfolio optimization finds its roots in the Modern Portfolio Theory (MPT) put forth by Harry Markowitz in the 1950s. MPT revolutionized the way investors think about portfolio construction, shifting focus from individual asset returns to overall portfolio performance. The theory introduced the idea of diversification, asserting that a well-diversified portfolio could reduce the risk without affecting expected returns.

MPT introduced two key concepts: expected return and risk, as measured by the standard deviation of returns. An 'efficient frontier' is formed by portfolios that offer the highest expected return for a given level of risk. Investors are then left to choose portfolios along this frontier, based on their risk tolerance.

Building an optimal portfolio involves more than just diversifying across assets. It requires understanding the correlations between asset returns. Assets that are perfectly positively correlated (a correlation coefficient of +1) move in sync with each other, while those perfectly negatively correlated (a correlation coefficient of -1) move in opposite directions. Assets with a correlation coefficient of 0 are said to have no correlation.

The magic of portfolio optimization lies in combining assets in such a way that the overall portfolio risk is reduced without impacting expected returns. This is achieved by adding assets to the portfolio that are less than perfectly correlated with the existing portfolio.

The mathematics of portfolio optimization involve complex optimization techniques. The goal is to maximize the portfolio's expected return for a given level of risk or to minimize risk for a given level of expected return. This can be expressed as an optimization problem with a constraint. In mathematical terms, it involves finding the weights of the assets in the portfolio that either maximizes the portfolio's expected return subject to a risk constraint or minimizes the portfolio's risk subject to a return constraint.

The exact solution to this optimization problem can be obtained using mathematical programming techniques such as quadratic programming. However, in practice, quants often resort to heuristic or numerical optimization methods such as gradient descent or genetic algorithms, especially when dealing with larger, more complex portfolios.

In the context of algorithmic trading, portfolio optimization takes on a more dynamic nature. Given that algorithmic trading strategies involve frequent buying and selling of assets, portfolio optimization becomes a continuous process. Traders must constantly rebalance their portfolios based on changing market conditions, asset prices, and trading signals generated by their algorithms.

In this setting, portfolio optimization methods often need to be adapted to accommodate transaction costs. Furthermore, the assumption of normally distributed returns, often used in MPT, may not hold, necessitating the use of more advanced techniques such as robust optimization or machine learning-based methods.

Case Study: Portfolio Optimization at Renaissance Technologies

Renaissance Technologies, the hedge fund founded by Jim Simons, is known for its emphasis on portfolio optimization. Its flagship Medallion fund has delivered exceptional returns over the years, largely due to its ability to optimize its portfolio effectively.

The fund's strategies involve trading a wide range of financial instruments, across various asset classes and geographies. Its success lies in its ability to identify uncorrelated trading signals and combine them into an optimal portfolio. By doing so, it has been able to deliver consistent returns even during turbulent market periods.

At the heart of Renaissance's portfolio optimization strategy is an intricate understanding of asset correlations and their dynamics. They have developed complex mathematical models that account for the non-linear and time-varying correlations between assets. These models allow them to dynamically rebalance their portfolio, minimizing risk and maximizing returns.

Their methods, while kept closely guarded, likely involve advanced machine learning techniques and high-frequency data, along with rigorous backtesting procedures. The successful application of these methods underscores the importance of portfolio optimization in algorithmic trading.

Traditional methods of portfolio optimization, like those based on MPT, work well under certain assumptions, but may fall short when dealing with more complex financial instruments or market conditions. For instance, they may not adequately capture extreme market events or the non-normal distribution of asset returns.

To address these challenges, advanced optimization techniques have been developed. These include:

Robust Optimization

Robust optimization methods are designed to perform well even when the underlying assumptions are not met. They provide solutions that are optimal under worst-case scenarios. In portfolio optimization, robust methods can help construct portfolios that perform well during extreme market conditions.

Stochastic Optimization

Stochastic optimization methods take into account the randomness in asset returns. These methods are particularly useful when dealing with assets whose returns are highly volatile or follow a complex stochastic process. Stochastic optimization can help build portfolios that are resilient to volatile market conditions.

Machine Learning in Portfolio Optimization

Machine learning methods, particularly reinforcement learning, have shown promise in portfolio optimization. These methods can learn complex patterns in asset returns and correlations, enabling the construction of more effective portfolios. Some researchers are exploring the use of deep reinforcement learning for dynamic portfolio optimization.

Portfolio optimization is a crucial aspect of algorithmic trading. It involves a blend of finance theory, mathematics, and computational methods. Whether you follow the principles of Modern Portfolio Theory or opt for advanced optimization techniques, building an optimal portfolio can significantly improve the performance of your algorithmic trading strategies.

Risk Management

Risk management is the beating heart of any successful algorithmic trading system. It's the guardian of your capital, the sentinel that watches over your profits and the shield that defends against catastrophic losses. At its core, risk management is about maintaining control and ensuring survival in the inherently uncertain and volatile world of financial markets.

Risk in financial markets is the possibility of losing money. It is an inherent part of investing and trading. Different types of risk include market risk (the risk of the overall market declining), credit risk (the risk of counterparty default), liquidity risk (the risk of not being able to buy or sell a position when needed), and operational risk (the risk of loss due to failed internal processes, people, or systems).

The first step in risk management is understanding the risks you are exposed to. This includes not only identifying the types of risk but also quantifying them. For algorithmic traders, this involves understanding how different market conditions could impact their trading algorithms and the potential loss that could result from it.

The Importance of a Risk Management Strategy

A comprehensive risk management strategy is a crucial component of a successful trading system. This strategy defines the rules and parameters for managing risk and guides your actions when faced with various market conditions.

The strategy should cover areas such as position sizing, stop-loss orders, risk diversification, risk monitoring, and stress testing. It should be dynamic, adjusting to changes in market conditions and the performance of the trading algorithm.

Risk Measures

There are various risk measures used by traders to quantify risk. These include:

Value-at-Risk (VaR)

VaR is a statistical measure of the risk of loss for a portfolio. It provides an estimate of the potential loss that could occur on a portfolio over a specific time period and at a given confidence level. VaR does not provide information about the potential loss beyond the VaR threshold.

Conditional Value-at-Risk (CVaR)

CVaR, also known as expected shortfall, is a measure of the risk of extreme losses. It provides an estimate of the expected loss on a portfolio in the worst-case scenarios that exceed the VaR threshold.

Drawdown

Drawdown measures the decline in the portfolio value from its peak to its trough over a specific period. It provides an indication of the loss that a trader had to endure during that period.

Risk Mitigation Strategies

Risk mitigation strategies aim to reduce the exposure to risk. These include:

Diversification

Diversification involves spreading investments across various assets or strategies to reduce exposure to any one of them. It helps mitigate unsystematic risk, the risk associated with individual assets or strategies.

Position Sizing

Position sizing involves determining the amount of capital to invest in each trade. Proper position sizing can help manage the risk of individual trades and prevent any single trade from having a disproportionate impact on the portfolio.

Stop-Loss Orders

Stop-loss orders are orders to sell an asset when its price reaches a certain level. They are designed to limit the loss on a position.

Case Study: Risk Management at Renaissance Technologies

Renaissance Technologies, a leading quantitative hedge fund, has an elaborate risk management system. Its risk management strategies are deeply integrated with its trading strategies and form a critical part of its overall success.

The firm employs sophisticated statistical models to quantify risk and uses advanced techniques to manage it. For instance, it uses machine learning methods to predict potential market crises and adjusts its portfolio accordingly. This proactive approach to risk management has helped the firm achieve exceptional returns while keeping risks in check.

Risk management is not an option but a necessity in algorithmic trading. With proper risk management, you can protect your capital, limit your losses, and survive to trade another day. The key is to understand the risks, quantify them, and then apply effective strategies to manage them. It's a continuous process that demands vigilance, discipline, and a deep understanding of markets and trading algorithms.

Risk Management Tools and Techniques

For algorithmic traders, managing risk involves employing a wide range of tools and techniques, from the relatively straightforward to the highly sophisticated.

Stress Testing

Stress testing is a simulation technique used to assess the potential impact of an extreme market event on a portfolio. It involves creating scenarios that reflect severe but plausible adverse market conditions and then determining how the portfolio would perform under those conditions.

Scenario Analysis

Closely related to stress testing, scenario analysis involves evaluating how a portfolio would respond to various hypothetical market conditions. This could involve changes in factors such as interest rates, exchange rates, commodity prices, or stock market indices.

Monte Carlo Simulations

Monte Carlo simulations are a type of computational algorithm that relies on repeated random sampling to estimate the probability of certain outcomes. In risk management, they can be used to simulate the behavior of an asset or portfolio and calculate the probability of different outcomes.

Beta

Beta is a measure of an investment's systematic risk, or its sensitivity to market movements. A beta of 1 indicates that the investment's price will move with the market, a beta less than 1 means the investment will be less volatile than the market, and a beta greater than 1 indicates the investment's price will be more volatile than the market.

Risk Management in Practice

Effective risk management is a balance between theoretical understanding and practical application. A firm understanding of the mathematics and concepts behind risk management is essential, but it's just as crucial to apply these concepts in a practical, flexible manner that suits your specific trading strategy and risk tolerance.

Take the example of stop-loss orders: while they are a useful tool for limiting losses, they can also result in trades being prematurely exited if they are not set at appropriate levels. As such, effective risk management involves not only understanding how to calculate appropriate stop-loss levels but also knowing when to adjust these levels based on changing market conditions or the performance of the trading algorithm.

Renaissance Technologies, with its blend of high-level quantitative analysis and nuanced understanding of market dynamics, provides a compelling example of this. It's not just about having the most advanced risk management tools; it's about knowing how to use them effectively.

Risk management is an essential aspect of successful algorithmic trading. It requires a blend of quantitative analysis, strategic thinking, and practical insight. Understanding the risks you face and adopting robust strategies to manage them will help you safeguard your trading capital and enhance the performance of your trading algorithms.

In the next chapter, we'll explore the concept of performance evaluation, another critical aspect of algorithmic trading. As we'll see, accurately measuring and interpreting the performance of your trading strategies is just as important as developing them in the first place.

CHAPTER 5: ALGORITHM DEVELOPMENT AND BACKTESTING

Introduction to Algorithm

Development

Algorithm development is the process of designing, implementing, and testing systematic trading strategies based on quantitative models, data-driven insights, and trading rules. The goal of algorithm development is to create a set of instructions or algorithms that can automatically execute trading decisions in a consistent and disciplined manner, minimizing the impact of emotions and human biases on trading performance. In this chapter, we will discuss the key steps and considerations in the algorithm development process, including:

1. Formulating a Trading Idea or Hypothesis
2. Data Preparation and Preprocessing
3. Feature Engineering and Selection
4. Model Development and Training
5. Trading Signal Generation and Execution
6. Risk Management and Position Sizing
7. Performance Evaluation and Optimization
8. Backtesting and Out-of-Sample Testing
9. Walk-Forward Analysis and Live Trading

Formulating a Trading Idea or Hypothesis

The first step in the algorithm development process is to formulate a trading idea or hypothesis based on market observations, quantitative analysis, or trading intuition. A trading idea can be a simple rule or pattern, such as buying when the price crosses above a moving average, or a more complex strategy based on statistical arbitrage, machine learning, or macroeconomic factors. When formulating a trading idea, it is important to consider the following factors:

- Market Efficiency and Alpha: Market efficiency is the degree to which market prices reflect all available information and adjust quickly to new information. In efficient markets, it is difficult to find persistent and exploitable trading opportunities, or alpha. When formulating a trading idea, it is important to consider the potential sources of alpha, such as market inefficiencies, behavioral biases, or structural factors, and assess their sustainability and scalability.

- Strategy Complexity and Robustness: Strategy complexity refers to the number of rules, parameters, or factors involved in a trading strategy. While more complex strategies may be able to capture subtle market patterns or relationships, they can also be more prone to overfitting and less robust in the face of changing market conditions. When formulating a trading idea, it is important to balance complexity and robustness and avoid relying on overly complex or data-driven models without a solid economic or theoretical rationale.

- Market Regime and Context: Market regimes are distinct periods or phases in the market characterized by different risk-return profiles, volatility levels, or market trends. Trading ideas or strategies may perform differently across different market regimes, and it is important to consider the market context and adaptability of a trading idea when developing an algorithmic trading strategy.

Data Preparation and Preprocessing

Data preparation and preprocessing are essential steps in the algorithm development process that involve acquiring, cleaning, and transforming the raw financial data needed for strategy development and testing. Data preparation and preprocessing can include the following tasks:

1. Data Acquisition: Data acquisition involves collecting the historical market data, such as price, volume, or fundamental data, needed to develop and test a trading strategy. Data can be obtained from various sources, such as commercial data providers, public data sources, or proprietary data feeds. It is important to ensure the quality, completeness, and accuracy of the data used in the algorithm development process, as errors or biases in the data can lead to false conclusions or poor strategy performance.

2. Data Cleaning: Data cleaning involves identifying and correcting errors, inconsistencies, or missing values in the raw financial data. This can include tasks such as removing duplicate records, filling in missing data, or adjusting for corporate actions, such as stock splits or dividends. Data cleaning is important for ensuring the reliability and validity of the strategy development and testing process.

3. Data Transformation: Data transformation involves converting the raw financial data into a suitable format or representation for strategy development and testing. This can include tasks such as resampling time series data to different frequencies (e.g., daily, weekly, or monthly), calculating returns or price changes, normalizing data to a common scale, or applying transformations, such as logarithms or differences, to stabilize the data or improve its statistical properties. Data transformation is important for ensuring the consistency and comparability of the data used in the algorithm development process.

Feature Engineering and Selection

Feature engineering is the process of creating input features or variables that can be used to develop and train quantitative trading models. Features can include technical indicators, fundamental factors, macroeconomic data, sentiment scores, or other derived variables that capture relevant market information or patterns. Feature selection involves choosing the most relevant and informative features for a trading strategy based on their predictive power, correlation, or other statistical criteria. Feature engineering and selection can involve the following tasks:

- Technical Indicators: Technical indicators are mathematical calculations based on price, volume, or other market data that can be used to identify trends, patterns, or trading signals in financial markets. Common technical indicators include moving averages, oscillators, such as the Relative Strength Index (RSI) or Stochastic Oscillator, and chart patterns, such as support and resistance levels, trendlines, or candlestick patterns.

- Fundamental Factors: Fundamental factors are financial ratios, metrics, or data points that can be used to analyze the financial health, valuation, or growth prospects of a company or investment. Examples of fundamental factors include earnings per share (EPS), price-to-earnings (P/E) ratio, dividend yield, or return on equity (ROE). Fundamental factors can be used to develop value, growth, or income-based trading strategies.

- Macroeconomic Data: Macroeconomic data includes economic indicators, such as GDP, inflation, interest rates, or employment data, that can be used to analyze the overall state of the economy or the performance of different sectors or industries. Macroeconomic data can be used to develop trading strategies based on economic trends, business cycles, or sector rotation.

- Sentiment Data: Sentiment data includes qualitative or quantitative measures of market sentiment, such as news sentiment scores, social media sentiment, analyst recommendations, or survey-based sentiment indicators, such as the Consumer Confidence Index or the Investor Sentiment Index. Sentiment data can be used to develop trading strategies based on market sentiment, contrarian indicators, or sentiment-driven events, such as earnings surprises or news-driven price reactions.

1. Feature Selection Methods: Feature selection methods are statistical techniques used to select the most relevant and informative features for a trading strategy based on their predictive power, correlation, or other criteria. Examples of feature selection methods include filter methods, such as correlation or mutual information-based selection, wrapper methods, such as forward or backward selection, or embedded methods, such as regularization or tree-based feature selection.

Model Development and Training

Model development and training involve designing and fitting quantitative trading models based on the selected features and trading ideas. This can include tasks such as:

1. Model Specification: Model specification involves choosing the appropriate model type, structure, or functional form for a trading strategy, such as linear regression, time series models, econometric models,

or machine learning models. Model specification is important for capturing the underlying relationships or patterns in the data and ensuring the robustness and generalizability of the trading strategy.

2. Model Training: Model training involves estimating the model parameters or weights based on the input features and target outputs (e.g., asset returns, price direction) using a set of training data. This can involve techniques such as ordinary least squares (OLS), maximum likelihood estimation (MLE), or gradient-based optimization for linear regression, time series, or machine learning models, respectively. Model training is important for fitting the trading model to the data and ensuring its predictive accuracy and stability.

3. Model Validation: Model validation involves assessing the performance and generalizability of a trading model by comparing its predictions or trading signals to the actual outcomes or market data. This can involve techniques such as cross-validation, holdout validation, or out-of-sample testing to evaluate the model's performance on different subsets of data or time periods. Model validation is important for ensuring the robustness and reliability of a trading strategy and avoiding overfitting or data snooping biases.

Trading Signal Generation and Execution

Trading signal generation involves using the trained trading model to generate buy, sell, or hold signals based on the input features and market data. Trading signal execution involves converting these signals into actual trade orders and managing the execution process, including order types, timing, and transaction costs. This can involve tasks such as:

- Order Types: Order types are instructions or conditions used to specify the price, quantity, or timing of a trade order, such as market orders, limit orders, stop orders, or trailing stop orders. Choosing the appropriate order type can help traders manage their market impact, slippage, and execution risk.

- Execution Algorithms: Execution algorithms are automated trading algorithms designed to optimize the trade execution process based on a specific objective, such as minimizing market impact, slippage, or transaction costs. Examples of execution algorithms include volume-weighted average price (VWAP) algorithms, time-weighted average price (TWAP) algorithms, or implementation shortfall algorithms.

- Transaction Costs and Market Impact: Transaction costs are the costs associated with executing a trade, such as bid-ask spreads, commissions, or market impact. Market impact refers to the effect of a trade on the market price, which can result in slippage or price impact for large orders or illiquid assets. Managing transaction costs and market impact is important for ensuring the profitability and scalability of an algorithmic trading strategy.

Risk Management and Position Sizing

Risk management and position sizing are essential components of algorithmic trading that involve managing the risks and performance of a trading portfolio. This can include tasks such as:

- Risk Measures and Metrics: As mentioned earlier, risk measures and metrics quantify the potential loss or uncertainty associated with a financial asset or portfolio. Examples of risk measures used in algorithmic trading include standard deviation, beta, Value-at-Risk (VaR), Conditional Value-at-Risk (CVaR), and maximum drawdown. These measures can help traders assess and manage the risks of their trading strategies and make informed portfolio allocation decisions.

- Position Sizing: Position sizing involves determining the optimal size or number of shares to trade based on a specific risk or capital allocation objective, such as fixed fractional, fixed dollar, or risk parity position sizing. Position sizing is important for managing the risk and diversification of a trading portfolio and ensuring the scalability and sustainability of a trading strategy.

Performance Evaluation and Optimization

Performance evaluation and optimization involve assessing the effectiveness and profitability of a trading strategy and optimizing its parameters, features, or rules to maximize its risk-adjusted performance. This can include tasks such as:

- Performance Metrics: As mentioned earlier, performance metrics are used to quantify the return, risk, or risk-adjusted performance of a trading strategy or portfolio. Examples of performance metrics include total return, annualized return, Sharpe ratio, Sortino ratio, Calmar ratio, and information ratio.

- Optimization Methods: Optimization methods are

mathematical techniques used to find the optimal values of a trading strategy's parameters, features, or rules based on a specific objective function, such as maximizing return, minimizing risk, or maximizing risk-adjusted performance. Examples of optimization methods used in algorithmic trading include grid search, gradient-based optimization, evolutionary algorithms, or Bayesian optimization.

Backtesting and Out-of-Sample Testing

Backtesting and out-of-sample testing are critical steps in the algorithm development process that involve evaluating the performance and robustness of a trading strategy using historical data. Backtesting involves simulating the historical performance of a trading strategy using a set of historical data, while out-of-sample testing involves evaluating the strategy's performance on a separate set of data that was not used in the strategy development process. These steps are crucial for ensuring the reliability, validity, and generalizability of a trading strategy and avoiding overfitting or data snooping biases.

- Backtesting: Backtesting involves simulating the historical performance of a trading strategy using a set of historical data to assess its profitability, risk, and robustness. This can involve calculating the strategy's returns, risk measures, and performance metrics, such as cumulative return, drawdowns, Sharpe ratio, or information ratio, and comparing its performance to a benchmark or reference portfolio. Backtesting can also involve testing the strategy's performance across different market regimes, asset classes, or time periods to assess its adaptability and generalizability.

- Out-of-Sample Testing: Out-of-sample testing involves

evaluating the performance of a trading strategy on a separate set of data that was not used in the strategy development process. This can involve partitioning the data into training, validation, and testing sets, or using rolling or expanding windows to simulate the real-time trading and updating process. Out-of-sample testing is important for validating the performance and generalizability of a trading strategy and avoiding overfitting or data snooping biases.

Walk-Forward Analysis and Live Trading

Walk-forward analysis is a more advanced form of out-of-sample testing that involves simulating the real-time trading and updating process of a trading strategy by iteratively training the model on a rolling or expanding window of data and testing its performance on a forward-looking window of data. Walk-forward analysis can provide a more realistic and robust assessment of a trading strategy's performance and adaptability in the face of changing market conditions and can help traders prepare for live trading.

- Walk-Forward Analysis: Walk-forward analysis involves simulating the real-time trading and updating process of a trading strategy by iteratively training the model on a rolling or expanding window of data and testing its performance on a forward-looking window of data. This can involve techniques such as rolling or expanding window cross-validation, walk-forward optimization, or out-of-sample model selection to assess the strategy's performance, stability, and adaptability.

- Live Trading: Live trading involves deploying and executing an algorithmic trading strategy on a live trading account or platform using real-time market data and order execution. Live trading can provide valuable insights into the real-world performance, transaction costs, and execution risks of a trading strategy and can help traders refine and improve their algorithms based on actual market conditions and feedback.

CHAPTER 6: EXECUTION AND ORDER MANAGEMENT

Execution and order management are crucial aspects of algorithmic trading that involve managing the trade execution process, including order types, timing, and transaction costs, to ensure the efficient and profitable execution of a trading strategy. In this chapter, we will discuss the key components of execution and order management, such as order types, execution algorithms, transaction costs, market impact, and execution risk, as well as best practices and techniques for optimizing trade execution and managing order flow.

Order Types

Order types are instructions or conditions used to specify the price, quantity, or timing of a trade order. Understanding and selecting the appropriate order type is essential for managing the trade execution process and controlling the market impact, slippage, and execution risk of a trading strategy. Some of the most common order types include:

- Market Orders: Market orders are instructions to buy or sell a security at the best available price in the market at the time the order is received. Market orders offer the advantage of immediate execution but can be subject to price uncertainty and slippage, especially for large orders or illiquid securities.

- Limit Orders: Limit orders are instructions to buy or sell a security at a specified price or better. Limit orders allow traders to control the price of their trades but can be subject to execution uncertainty, as the order will only be executed if the specified price is reached.

- Stop Orders: Stop orders, also known as stop-loss orders, are instructions to buy or sell a security once the market price reaches a specified level. Stop orders can be used to protect a position from excessive losses or to enter a position once a specific price level is breached, but can be subject to price uncertainty and slippage if the stop price is triggered in a fast-moving or illiquid market.

- Trailing Stop Orders: Trailing stop orders are a type of stop order that adjusts the stop price based on the market price or a specified trailing amount. Trailing stop orders can be used to lock in profits or limit losses on a position as the market price moves in a favorable direction but can be subject to the same price uncertainty and slippage as regular stop orders.

- Conditional Orders: Conditional orders are instructions to buy or sell a security based on specific conditions or criteria, such as the price of another security, the occurrence of an event, or the passage of a certain time period. Conditional orders can be used to implement more complex trading strategies or to manage the execution of multiple orders in a coordinated manner.

Execution Algorithms

Execution algorithms are automated trading algorithms designed to optimize the trade execution process based on a specific objective, such as minimizing market impact, slippage, or transaction costs. Execution algorithms can help traders manage their order flow more efficiently and achieve better execution outcomes by intelligently splitting, timing, or routing their orders. Some of the most common execution algorithms include:

- Volume-Weighted Average Price (VWAP) Algorithms: VWAP algorithms are designed to achieve the volume-weighted average price of a security over a specified time period by breaking the order into smaller sub-orders and executing them at intervals that match the security's historical volume distribution. VWAP algorithms can help traders minimize their market impact and achieve a benchmark price that is representative of the security's trading activity.

- Time-Weighted Average Price (TWAP) Algorithms:

TWAP algorithms are designed to achieve the time-weighted average price of a security over a specified time period by breaking the order into smaller sub-orders and executing them at regular time intervals. TWAP algorithms can help traders minimize their market impact and achieve a benchmark price that is representative of the security's trading activity over time.

- Implementation Shortfall Algorithms: Implementation shortfall algorithms are designed to minimize the difference between the actual execution price of a trade and the decision price at which the trade was initiated, also known as the implementation shortfall. These algorithms aim to minimize the combination of market impact, slippage, and delay costs by dynamically adjusting the execution strategy based on real-time market conditions, liquidity, and trading signals. Implementation shortfall algorithms can help traders balance the trade-off between execution speed and execution costs to achieve an optimal execution outcome.

- Liquidity-Seeking Algorithms: Liquidity-seeking algorithms are designed to search for and execute trades in hidden or less visible liquidity sources, such as dark pools, alternative trading systems (ATSs), or reserve or hidden orders on exchanges. Liquidity-seeking algorithms can help traders minimize their market impact and access additional liquidity by intelligently routing their orders to multiple venues or executing them in a stealthy manner.

- Adaptive Algorithms: Adaptive algorithms are designed to dynamically adjust their execution strategy based on real-time market conditions, trading signals, or user-defined parameters. Adaptive algorithms can help traders optimize their execution performance and respond to changing market conditions, such as changes in liquidity, volatility, or market trends.

Transaction Costs and Market Impact

Transaction costs are the costs associated with executing a trade, such as bid-ask spreads, commissions, or market impact. Managing transaction costs is important for ensuring the profitability and scalability of an algorithmic trading strategy, as these costs can erode the returns of a trading strategy and affect its risk-adjusted performance. Some of the key factors and considerations related to transaction costs and market impact include:

- Bid-Ask Spreads: Bid-ask spreads are the difference between the best bid (buy) and best ask (sell) prices in the market and represent the cost of trading a security due to market liquidity and market maker competition. Wider bid-ask spreads can increase the transaction costs and price uncertainty of a trade, especially for illiquid securities or large orders.

- Commissions: Commissions are fees charged by brokers or trading platforms for executing a trade or providing other services, such as market data, clearing, or settlement. Commissions can vary depending on the broker, trading platform, security, or order type and can impact the profitability and scalability of a trading strategy, especially for high-frequency or high-turnover strategies.

- Market Impact: Market impact refers to the effect of a trade on the market price, which can result in slippage or price impact for large orders or illiquid assets.

Market impact can be influenced by factors such as order size, order type, execution speed, and market liquidity and can affect the execution performance and profitability of a trading strategy. Managing market impact is important for minimizing the transaction costs and information leakage associated with a trade and achieving better execution outcomes.

Execution Risk

Execution risk refers to the uncertainties and potential losses associated with the trade execution process, such as price uncertainty, slippage, incomplete or partial execution, or counterparty risk. Managing execution risk is important for ensuring the reliability and profitability of an algorithmic trading strategy and avoiding unwanted exposures or losses. Some of the key factors and considerations related to execution risk include:

- Price Uncertainty: Price uncertainty refers to the potential for the actual execution price of a trade to deviate from the expected or desired price due to factors such as market volatility, liquidity, or order type. Managing price uncertainty is important for achieving better execution outcomes and minimizing the risk of adverse price movements or slippage.

- Slippage: Slippage refers to the difference between the expected execution price of a trade and the actual execution price, which can result from factors such as price uncertainty, market impact, or order execution delays. Slippage can erode the returns of a trading strategy and affect its risk-adjusted performance, especially for high-frequency or high-turnover strategies.

- Incomplete or Partial Execution: Incomplete or partial

execution refers to the risk that a trade order may not be fully executed at the desired price or quantity due to factors such as order size, liquidity, or order type. Managing incomplete or partial execution is important for ensuring the proper execution of a trading strategy and avoiding unwanted exposures or imbalances in a portfolio.

- Counterparty Risk: Counterparty risk refers to the risk that a counterparty, such as a broker, exchange, or clearinghouse, may fail to fulfill its obligations or perform its services, which can result in losses or disruptions for a trading strategy. Managing counterparty risk is important for ensuring the reliability and stability of an algorithmic trading strategy and avoiding potential losses or disruptions due to counterparty failures or insolvencies.

Best Practices and Techniques for Execution and Order Management

- Optimize Order Types and Execution Algorithms: Selecting the appropriate order type and execution algorithm can help manage the trade execution process more efficiently and achieve better execution outcomes by controlling market impact, slippage, and execution risk.

- Monitor and Manage Transaction Costs: Monitoring and managing transaction costs, such as bid-ask spreads, commissions, or market impact, can help ensure the profitability and scalability of an algorithmic trading strategy and improve its risk-adjusted performance.

- Diversify Order Routing and Liquidity Sources: Diversifying order routing and liquidity sources, such as using multiple exchanges, brokers, or alternative trading systems (ATSs), can help access additional liquidity, minimize market impact, and reduce counterparty risk.

- Employ Risk Management Techniques: Employing risk management techniques, such as position sizing, stop orders, or risk controls, can help manage execution risk and protect a trading strategy from excessive losses or unwanted exposures.

- Monitor and Review Execution Performance: Monitoring and reviewing execution performance, such as analyzing trade fills, execution quality, or performance metrics, can help identify potential issues or areas for improvement in the trade execution process and refine the execution strategy or algorithms.

Liquidity and order routing

Introduction to Liquidity

Liquidity is a crucial aspect of financial markets, as it reflects the ease with which assets can be bought or sold without significantly impacting their prices. It is a vital component of market efficiency, enabling participants to execute trades rapidly and with minimal transaction costs. In essence, a liquid market is characterized by a high level of trading activity, narrow bid-ask spreads, and minimal price impact from individual trades.

Factors Influencing Liquidity

Several factors can influence the liquidity of a financial instrument or market:

- Market Participants: The number and diversity of

market participants, including institutional investors, hedge funds, market makers, and individual traders, contribute to liquidity by providing a continuous flow of buy and sell orders.

- Trading Volume: Higher trading volume typically results in increased liquidity, as it indicates that more participants are actively buying and selling the asset in question.

- Market Transparency: Transparency refers to the availability of information about the asset or market, such as price quotes, trading volumes, and order book data. Greater transparency can facilitate more informed decision-making and improve market participants' ability to assess liquidity.

- Market Structure: The structure of a market, including the organization of exchanges, trading platforms, and clearing and settlement systems, can influence liquidity by affecting the ease and efficiency with which trades can be executed.

Order Routing and its Role in Liquidity Management

Order routing is the process by which buy and sell orders are directed to the appropriate trading venues for execution. Effective order routing is critical for achieving optimal trade execution, as it helps traders access the best available liquidity sources, minimize transaction costs, and reduce market impact.

Order Routing Strategies

There are several strategies that traders can employ to optimize their order routing and liquidity management:

- Smart Order Routing (SOR): Smart order routing algorithms analyze multiple market venues in real-time to identify the best available liquidity and price opportunities. SOR can help traders access fragmented liquidity across various exchanges, alternative trading systems (ATSs), and dark pools, thus improving execution quality and reducing transaction costs.

- Algorithmic Trading: Algorithmic trading strategies can incorporate order routing decisions as part of their overall logic. By dynamically adjusting order routing based on real-time market conditions, liquidity, and trading signals, these algorithms can help traders optimize their execution performance and respond to changing market conditions.

- Direct Market Access (DMA): Direct market access allows traders to bypass intermediaries, such as brokers or market makers, and directly interact with the order book of an exchange or trading platform. DMA can help traders reduce transaction costs, increase control over their order execution, and improve their ability to access liquidity.

Challenges and Considerations in Order Routing and Liquidity Management

Effective order routing and liquidity management can be complex and challenging, as traders need to navigate a diverse and constantly evolving financial market landscape. Some key considerations include:

- Market Fragmentation: As financial markets have become increasingly fragmented, with multiple trading venues offering access to the same or similar assets, traders must carefully consider their order routing decisions to ensure they access the best available liquidity and prices.

- Information Leakage: When routing orders across various trading venues, traders may risk exposing their trading intentions, leading to information leakage that can impact prices and liquidity. To mitigate this risk, traders can employ techniques such as iceberg orders, which partially conceal the total order size, or utilize dark pools to execute trades without publicly displaying their orders.

- Regulatory Compliance: Regulatory requirements, such as best execution obligations or restrictions on accessing certain liquidity sources, can impact traders' order routing decisions and liquidity management strategies. Traders should be aware of and adhere to relevant regulations in their respective jurisdictions.

By understanding and managing the various components of the trade execution process, such as order types, execution algorithms, transaction costs, market impact, and execution risk, traders can optimize their trade execution and order management practices to achieve better execution outcomes and improve the overall performance and profitability of their algorithmic trading strategies.

CHAPTER 7: INFRASTRUCTURE AND TECHNOLOGY

The infrastructure and technology underpinning an algorithmic trading system are essential for its successful operation, as they provide the foundation upon which trading strategies are built and executed. In this section, we will explore the key components of an algorithmic trading system's infrastructure and technology, including hardware and networking requirements, software and programming languages, and APIs and trading platforms.

Hardware and Networking Requirements

A robust and efficient hardware infrastructure is crucial for algorithmic trading, as it can significantly impact the system's performance, reliability, and latency. Key hardware components and networking requirements include:

Computing Power

High-performance computing resources are essential for running complex trading algorithms and processing large volumes of market data in real-time. Algorithmic traders should consider the following factors when selecting their computing hardware:

- Processor: A powerful central processing unit (CPU) is vital for executing trading algorithms and performing complex calculations quickly.

- Memory: Sufficient random-access memory (RAM) is necessary for storing and processing large datasets, such as historical price data or order book information.

- Graphics Processing Unit (GPU): GPUs can accelerate certain mathematical computations, making them a valuable resource for some algorithmic trading strategies, particularly those involving machine learning or other computationally-intensive tasks.

Network Connectivity

Low-latency network connectivity is crucial for algorithmic

trading, as it enables traders to rapidly access market data and execute trades with minimal delays. Key networking considerations include:

- Internet Connection: A high-speed, low-latency internet connection is essential for connecting to trading platforms, exchanges, and data providers.
- Co-location: Co-locating trading servers in close proximity to an exchange's servers can help reduce latency by minimizing the physical distance that data must travel.
- Network Infrastructure: Optimized network hardware, such as routers, switches, and network interface cards (NICs), can help ensure efficient data transmission and minimize latency.

Software and Programming Languages

The choice of software and programming languages can significantly impact the development, implementation, and performance of algorithmic trading strategies. Key considerations include:

Programming Languages

Selecting the right programming language for an algorithmic trading system depends on factors such as performance, ease of use, and compatibility with existing infrastructure. Popular programming languages for algorithmic trading include:

- Python: Python is a versatile, high-level programming language that offers a rich ecosystem of libraries and tools for data analysis, machine learning, and algorithmic trading.

- **C++:** C++ is a high-performance, compiled programming language that is well-suited for low-latency trading applications, as it allows for greater control over system resources and performance.

- **Java:** Java is a widely-used, object-oriented programming language that offers a strong balance of performance and ease of use, making it a popular choice for many algorithmic traders.

- **R:** R is a statistical programming language that is particularly well-suited for data analysis, modeling, and visualization tasks.

Trading Platforms and Software Tools

A variety of trading platforms and software tools are available to facilitate the development and execution of algorithmic trading strategies. These can include:

- **Integrated Development Environments (IDEs):** IDEs, such as Visual Studio Code, PyCharm, or RStudio, can streamline the development process by providing a unified workspace for writing, debugging, and testing code.

- **Backtesting and Simulation Platforms:** Platforms such as QuantConnect, Quantopian, or NinjaTrader allow traders to test and refine their strategies using historical market data.

- **Risk Management and Portfolio Optimization Tools:** Software tools like Riskalyze or Portfolio Visualizer can help traders assess and manage the risk and performance of their trading strategies.

APIs and Trading Platforms

Application programming interfaces (APIs) are essential for integrating algorithmic trading systems with external data sources, trading platforms, and other software tools. APIs enable the efficient exchange of data and instructions between different software components, allowing traders to access market data, submit orders, and manage their positions programmatically.

Data APIs

Data APIs provide access to a variety of market data sources, including historical price data, real-time quotes, and fundamental financial information. Popular data APIs include:

- Quandl: Quandl offers a wide range of financial and economic data, including historical stock prices, futures, options, and economic indicators.

- Alpha Vantage: Alpha Vantage provides access to historical and real-time stock quotes, technical indicators, and other market data.

- Intrinio: Intrinio offers a comprehensive suite of financial data APIs, covering historical and real-time pricing, financial statements, and other fundamental data.

Trading Platform APIs

Trading platform APIs enable algorithmic traders to interface directly with exchanges, brokers, and other trading venues, allowing them to manage their orders and positions programmatically. Some popular trading platform APIs include:

- Interactive Brokers: The Interactive Brokers API offers access to a broad range of financial instruments and markets, including stocks, futures, options, and forex.

- Alpaca: Alpaca is a commission-free trading platform

that offers a REST API for stock trading, allowing developers to build and deploy algorithmic trading strategies.

- MetaTrader: MetaTrader is a popular trading platform for forex and CFD trading, offering a proprietary scripting language (MQL) and API for developing and deploying algorithmic trading strategies.

Building a robust and efficient algorithmic trading system requires a comprehensive understanding of the underlying infrastructure and technology components and by considering hardware and networking requirements, selecting appropriate software and programming languages, and leveraging APIs and trading platforms, traders can develop and implement algorithmic strategies that maximize performance, minimize latency, and adapt to evolving market conditions.

The table below provides a snapshot of the diverse tools available to the algorithmic trader. Each platform or tool has its own strengths, and the best fit would depend on the specific needs of the trader or institution.

Platform/Tool	Description
MetaTrader 4/5	Widely-used retail forex trading platform offering automated trading capabilities via its proprietary scripting language, MQL4/5. Supports algorithmic strategies and custom indicators.
NinjaTrader	Platform offering advanced charting, backtesting, and trade simulation. Known for its C#-based automated trading system and extensive market analytics tools.

QuantConnect	Cloud-based algorithmic trading platform that provides its users with free access to financial data and cloud computing. Supports C#, Python, and F#.
Quantopian	(Note: As of 2021, they ceased operations for individual users) A cloud-based platform that allowed users to write Python algorithms, backtest them on historical data, and connect to brokerages.
AlgoTrader	Comprehensive algorithmic trading software for quantitative hedge funds to trading cryptocurrencies, equities, and forex. Allows for automated order execution.
TradeStation	Known for its brokerage services, but also offers a powerful trading platform suitable for testing, optimizing, and executing automated strategies.
cAlgo	Built to be an accompanying platform for cTrader, allowing for the development of algorithms and technical indicators.
Backtrader	Python-based, open-source backtesting platform that also supports live trading across various brokerages.
Zipline	Open-source, Python-based algorithmic trading simulator that powers Quantopian. Notable for its capability to handle large datasets and for its performance analytics

	features.
Interactive Brokers (IB) API	Known for its brokerage services, IB also offers APIs that allow traders to automate their strategies, request market data, and place orders.
ThinkOrSwim API	A platform by TD Ameritrade that offers an API for algorithmic trading, leveraging its advanced trading tools and charts.

CHAPTER 8: REGULATORY AND COMPLIANCE CONSIDERATIONS

Algorithmic trading, like any other financial activity, is subject to a range of regulatory and compliance requirements. These rules are designed to protect market participants, maintain the integrity of the financial system, and prevent market abuse. In this chapter, we will explore some of the key regulatory and compliance considerations that algorithmic traders must take into account when developing and deploying their trading strategies.

Regulatory Frameworks

Algorithmic trading is regulated by various financial authorities around the world, each with its own set of rules and requirements. Some of the major regulatory frameworks governing algorithmic trading include:

United States

In the United States, algorithmic trading is regulated primarily by the Securities and Exchange Commission (SEC) and the Commodity Futures Trading Commission (CFTC). Key regulations affecting algorithmic traders include:

- Regulation National Market System (Reg NMS): Reg NMS is a set of rules designed to modernize and strengthen the U.S. national market system for equity securities. It includes provisions related to order routing, best execution, and market data access, which can impact algorithmic trading strategies.

- Market Access Rule (SEC Rule 15c3-5): This rule requires broker-dealers to establish, document, and maintain a system of risk management controls and supervisory procedures to prevent the entry of erroneous orders and ensure compliance with regulatory requirements.

- CFTC Regulation Automated Trading (Reg AT): Reg AT is a set of proposed rules aimed at increasing transparency and reducing risk in automated trading activities in the futures markets. It includes provisions related to pre-trade risk controls, algorithmic trading source code retention, and registration requirements for certain algorithmic traders.

European Union

In the European Union, algorithmic trading is governed by the Markets in Financial Instruments Directive II (MiFID II) and the accompanying Markets in Financial Instruments Regulation (MiFIR). Key provisions affecting algorithmic traders include:

- Algorithmic Trading Definition and Requirements: MiFID II defines algorithmic trading and imposes a range of requirements on firms engaged in this activity, such as the establishment of systems and controls to prevent market abuse and ensure compliance with regulatory obligations.

- Market Making and High-Frequency Trading: MiFID II introduces specific requirements for firms engaged in market making or high-frequency trading, including mandatory registration, continuous quoting obligations, and the provision of liquidity on a consistent basis.

- Transaction Reporting: MiFID II imposes extensive transaction reporting requirements on firms engaged in algorithmic trading, with the aim of increasing transparency and improving market surveillance.

Compliance Considerations

Algorithmic traders must ensure that their strategies and operations comply with the relevant regulatory requirements. Key compliance considerations include:

Pre-Trade Risk Controls

Implementing pre-trade risk controls is essential to prevent the submission of erroneous orders and ensure compliance with position and order size limits. These controls may include price collars, maximum order size limits, and position limits, among others.

Monitoring and Surveillance

Algorithmic traders must establish systems and processes for monitoring and surveillance to detect and prevent potential market abuse, such as market manipulation or insider trading. This may involve the use of automated surveillance tools, regular reviews of trading activity, and the establishment of a robust compliance function.

Record-Keeping and Reporting

Regulatory frameworks often require algorithmic traders to maintain records of their trading activities, including order and trade data, algorithmic trading source code, and documentation of risk management controls and procedures. Additionally, traders may be subject to transaction reporting requirements, which involve the submission of detailed trade information to regulatory authorities.

CHAPTER 9: BUILDING A SUCCESSFUL ALGORITHMIC TRADING BUSINESS

Building a successful algorithmic trading business requires more than just the technical knowledge of implementing effective trading strategies. It also involves developing a competitive edge, protecting intellectual property, managing talent, and continuously researching and improving your strategies. In this chapter, we will discuss these critical aspects and provide guidance on how to build a thriving algorithmic trading business.

Developing a Competitive Edge

In the highly competitive world of algorithmic trading, having a competitive edge is crucial for success. A competitive edge can come from various sources, such as superior technology, unique data, or innovative trading strategies. Here are some ways to develop a competitive edge:

Cutting-edge Technology

Investing in cutting-edge technology can help your algorithmic trading business stay ahead of the competition. This may involve using high-performance computing infrastructure, low-latency networking, and advanced software tools. By leveraging state-of-the-art technology, you can increase the speed, efficiency, and performance of your trading strategies.

Unique Data Sources

Access to unique or proprietary data sources can provide valuable insights and help you develop innovative trading strategies. This may include alternative data, such as social media sentiment, satellite imagery, or web scraping, which can complement traditional financial data sources.

Innovative Trading Strategies

Developing innovative and proprietary trading strategies is key to achieving a competitive edge. This involves continuous research and development, rigorous backtesting, and a disciplined approach to strategy implementation. By creating trading strategies that exploit market inefficiencies, you can generate consistent returns and differentiate yourself from other market participants.

Intellectual Property Protection

Protecting your intellectual property (IP) is critical to the long-term success of your algorithmic trading business. Your IP may include trading algorithms, proprietary data, and other valuable assets. Here are some ways to protect your intellectual property:

Non-disclosure Agreements

Using non-disclosure agreements (NDAs) can help protect your intellectual property when sharing sensitive information with third parties, such as employees, contractors, or partners. NDAs legally bind the receiving party to keep the information confidential and prevent unauthorized use or disclosure.

Trade Secret Protection

Trade secret protection involves maintaining the confidentiality of valuable information, such as trading algorithms and data sources, by taking reasonable steps to prevent unauthorized access or disclosure. This may include implementing strong access controls, using secure communication channels, and regularly auditing your security measures.

Patent Protection

In some cases, it may be possible to protect your intellectual property through patents. While the patentability of trading algorithms can be challenging, certain aspects of your trading system, such as data processing techniques or software tools, may be eligible for patent protection. Consulting with an IP attorney can help you determine if patent protection is appropriate for your business.

Team Building and Talent Management

Having the right team in place is essential for the success of your algorithmic trading business. A skilled and diverse team can help you develop innovative trading strategies, manage risk, and navigate the complex world of finance. Here are some tips for building and managing a successful team:

Hiring the Right Talent

Recruit individuals with a diverse range of skills and backgrounds, including quantitative researchers, software engineers, and risk managers. Look for candidates with strong problem-solving abilities, a passion for finance, and a willingness to learn and adapt.

Providing Training and Development Opportunities

Invest in the professional development of your team by offering training programs, mentorship opportunities, and resources for continuous learning. Encourage your team members to stay up-to-date with the latest advancements in finance, technology, and data science, and foster a culture of collaboration and knowledge sharing.

Performance Management and Incentives

Establish clear performance goals and regularly evaluate the performance of your team members. Provide feedback and support to help them improve and grow within the organization. Implement a fair and transparent incentive structure that rewards top performers and aligns their interests with the success of the business.

Continuous Research and Improvement

In the ever-evolving world of finance, staying ahead of the competition requires constant research and improvement of your trading strategies and systems. Here are some best practices for ensuring continuous growth and success:

Rigorous Backtesting and Validation

Regularly backtest and validate your trading strategies using historical and out-of-sample data. This will help you identify potential weaknesses, assess the robustness of your strategies, and make improvements as necessary.

Adapting to Changing Market Conditions

Financial markets are dynamic and can change rapidly due to various factors, such as economic events, regulatory changes, or shifts in investor sentiment. Continuously monitor market conditions and be prepared to adjust your trading strategies and risk management practices as needed.

Research and Collaboration

Encourage a culture of research and collaboration within your organization. Allocate resources for research projects, organize internal workshops and presentations, and promote collaboration between team members with diverse skill sets and expertise.

Staying Informed

Stay informed about the latest developments in finance, technology, and data science by attending conferences, participating in industry forums, and engaging with relevant research publications. Leverage new insights and knowledge to enhance your trading strategies and systems.

Building a successful algorithmic trading business involves developing a competitive edge, protecting your intellectual property, building, and managing a talented team, and continuously researching and improving your strategies. By focusing on these critical aspects and maintaining a disciplined approach to strategy implementation and risk management, you can build a thriving algorithmic trading business that generates consistent returns and stands the test of time.

CHAPTER 10: ADVANCED TOPICS IN QUANTITATIVE TRADING

Quantitative trading stands on the frontier of technological advancement and financial theory. As we venture into the advanced topics of this field, we immerse ourselves in the latest innovations and complex strategies that define elite quant trading firms.

This chapter navigates through the high-dimensional space where mathematics, computer science, and economic theory converge. We begin by exploring the intricate models of algorithmic arbitrage, where discrepancies across markets and assets are identified and exploited by sophisticated algorithms. The discussion then shifts to the realm of high-frequency trading, a domain where speed and precision are paramount, and where the infrastructure's technological prowess can provide a competitive edge.

We delve into the complexities of predictive analytics, where big data and machine learning algorithms forecast market movements with uncanny accuracy. Here, we dissect the algorithms that parse through vast datasets, extracting patterns and insights invisible to the human eye.

Quantitative risk management also takes center stage, as we examine the stochastic calculus and econometric models that underpin the rigorous assessment and mitigation of financial risks. This section elucidates on the latest advancements in portfolio optimization, including the use of machine learning techniques to manage and diversify risk in unprecedented ways.

The chapter culminates with an exploration of the ethical and regulatory considerations in quantitative trading. As algorithms assume greater control over market dynamics, we contemplate the implications for market fairness, stability, and integrity. We consider the evolving regulatory landscape, ensuring that our advanced trading strategies not only pursue profitability but also uphold the highest standards of market conduct.

In this journey through advanced quantitative trading, we not only aim to enlighten but also to inspire innovation and prudence in equal measure. As the markets continue to evolve, so too must the quant trader's arsenal of strategies and tools—always advancing, always adapting.

Algorithmic Arbitrage in Quantitative Trading

Algorithmic arbitrage represents the quintessence of quantitative trading. Sophisticated algorithms scan multiple markets and assets simultaneously, identifying price discrepancies that can be exploited for profit. These models operate on the principle of purchasing an asset at a lower price in one market and selling it at a higher price in another, capturing the spread between the two. This strategy requires advanced statistical models and ultra-fast execution, as arbitrage opportunities can vanish within fractions of a second.

Algorithmic arbitrage exploits price discrepancies between markets or financial instruments. These strategies involve complex mathematical models that quickly identify and act upon opportunities for risk-free profits. In practice, they rely on advanced computational technologies and high-speed data feeds to monitor multiple trading venues simultaneously.

One common type of algorithmic arbitrage is statistical arbitrage, which uses statistical methods to identify pairs of assets whose prices have historically moved together. When the price movement diverges, the algorithm will short the overperforming asset and buy the underperforming one, betting on the reversion to their mean historical relationship.

Another form is triangular arbitrage, used in foreign exchange markets, which takes advantage of currency pairs' mispricing. An algorithm can execute a series of trades that capitalizes on differences in exchange rates for three or more currencies to lock in a risk-free profit.

Merger arbitrage algorithms monitor and trade stocks of companies involved in pending mergers or acquisitions, aiming to profit from the price convergence of the acquiring and target company shares.

For each of these strategies, the algorithm must account for transaction costs, latency, and the potential impact of trades on market prices. The goal is to execute trades that capture the arbitrage opportunity before it disappears, which can occur within milliseconds.

The success of algorithmic arbitrage hinges on the speed and efficiency of the algorithm, as well as access to fast and reliable market data. As such, these strategies are often employed by well-capitalized institutional traders, such as hedge funds and proprietary trading firms, who can invest in the necessary technological infrastructure.

Algorithmic arbitrage has grown more complex with the advent of diverse financial products and global trading platforms. Cross-market arbitrage algorithms continuously analyze price differences for the same asset traded on different exchanges, while cross-asset strategies look for mispricings between related instruments, such as ETFs and the basket of underlying stocks.

Latency arbitrage has emerged with advancements in technology, where traders use ultra-low latency connections to exploit price differences arising from delays in price quotes between exchanges. However, this practice has led to significant discussions regarding market fairness and the ethical use of technology in trading.

The efficiency of these arbitrage algorithms depends not just on speed but also on the sophistication of the models, which must account for a multitude of factors, such as market liquidity, order execution speed, and the temporary market impact of trades. As markets evolve and regulatory frameworks adapt, algorithmic arbitrage remains a dynamic and challenging field that continues to offer opportunities for those with the technological edge and quantitative expertise.

The domain of algorithmic arbitrage is expanding into the exploitation of discrepancies in real-time across a globalized market. Algorithms are now designed to be adaptive, learning from market dynamics to optimize trading paths and timing. Sophistication in these algorithms encompasses not just statistical models but also elements of machine learning, which allow for predictive rather than reactive arbitrage strategies. The complexity of these systems cannot be overstated, as they must manage vast datasets, account for the geopolitical impact on markets, and adjust to regulatory changes—all at speeds incomprehensible to the human trader. As we move forward, the intersection of data science, advanced mathematics, and financial expertise is likely to become even more profound, continually reshaping the landscape of quantitative trading.

Pseudocode for a Simple Statistical Arbitrage Algorithm

Define the pair of stocks

stock_A = 'Stock_A_Ticker'

```
stock_B = 'Stock_B_Ticker'

# Fetch historical price data for both stocks
prices_A = get_historical_prices(stock_A)
prices_B = get_historical_prices(stock_B)

# Calculate the historical price ratio
price_ratio = prices_A / prices_B

# Determine the mean and standard deviation of the price ratio
mean_ratio = mean(price_ratio)
std_dev_ratio = std(price_ratio)

# Trading logic
if current_price_ratio > mean_ratio + (2 * std_dev_ratio):
    # Price ratio is above 2 standard deviations - sell Stock A, buy Stock B
    place_order(sell, stock_A)
    place_order(buy, stock_B)
elif current_price_ratio < mean_ratio - (2 * std_dev_ratio):
    # Price ratio is below 2 standard deviations - buy Stock A, sell Stock B
    place_order(buy, stock_A)
    place_order(sell, stock_B)
```

```
# Pseudocode for a Simple Statistical Arbitrage Algorithm

# Define the pair of stocks
stock_A = 'Stock_A_Ticker'
stock_B = 'Stock_B_Ticker'

# Fetch historical price data for both stocks
prices_A = get_historical_prices(stock_A)
prices_B = get_historical_prices(stock_B)

# Calculate the historical price ratio
price_ratio = prices_A / prices_B

# Determine the mean and standard deviation of the price ratio
mean_ratio = mean(price_ratio)
std_dev_ratio = std(price_ratio)

# Trading logic
if current_price_ratio > mean_ratio + (2 * std_dev_ratio):
    # Price ratio is above 2 standard deviations - sell Stock A, buy Stock B
    place_order(sell, stock_A)
    place_order(buy, stock_B)
elif current_price_ratio < mean_ratio - (2 * std_dev_ratio):
    # Price ratio is below 2 standard deviations - buy Stock A, sell Stock B
    place_order(buy, stock_A)
```

High-Frequency Trading (HFT)

High-frequency trading (HFT) is a field characterized by algorithms executing a large number of orders at very fast speeds. HFT strategies thrive on minute, short-lived market inefficiencies, requiring state-of-the-art technology and sophisticated algorithms to detect and act upon such opportunities rapidly. Speed is of the essence, with firms investing heavily in network infrastructure and colocation services to minimize latency. HFT has not only revolutionized the market's structure but also sparked debate on market fairness and the need for regulation.

High-Frequency Trading (HFT) operates on the edge of speed, using algorithms, powerful computers, and low-latency data networks to execute trades within fractions of a second. It's a domain where firms compete not just on strategy, but on sheer technological prowess.

HFT strategies are diverse, yet they share a common goal: to capitalize on small, short-term market inefficiencies. These inefficiencies can come from simple bid-ask spreads, market-making, event arbitrage, statistical arbitrage, and more. HFT firms might also employ news-based trading, where algorithms parse news feeds and execute trades based on the information faster than any human could.

Critics of HFT argue that it can lead to market instability and benefit a select few with the resources to compete at these speeds. Proponents, however, argue that HFT adds liquidity to the markets, narrowing spreads and allowing for more efficient price discovery.

In exploring HFT, we will also delve into the infrastructure that enables its rapid execution: direct market access, colocation services, and the sophisticated use of dark pools. We also examine the regulatory landscape shaping HFT practices, including measures like the 'Volcker Rule' and the 'Tick Size Pilot Program' in the U.S.

The infrastructure enabling High-Frequency Trading (HFT) is as sophisticated as the algorithms it supports. Direct Market Access (DMA) allows HFT firms to interact directly with the exchange's order book, bypassing traditional brokerage channels. This direct connection is crucial for minimizing latency.

Colocation services are another cornerstone. By hosting their servers physically close to the exchange's data centers, HFT firms can execute trades at incredibly high speeds. The proximity reduces the time it takes for data to travel, giving a significant advantage in a realm where milliseconds can make a difference.

The use of dark pools is also prevalent in HFT. These private exchanges or forums for trading securities allow participants to execute large orders without exposing their intention to the public market, thus minimizing market impact.

On the regulatory front, HFT practices are shaped by several key measures. The Volcker Rule, part of the Dodd-Frank Wall Street Reform and Consumer Protection Act, restricts the ways banks can invest, limiting proprietary trading and eliminating certain relationships with hedge funds and private equity funds. The Tick Size Pilot Program was a test initiated by the U.S. Securities and Exchange Commission (SEC) to see if increasing the tick size for small-cap stocks would improve market quality.

These regulatory measures reflect ongoing efforts to ensure fair and stable markets in the face of rapidly evolving trading technologies. The challenge for regulators is to maintain a balance between fostering innovation and protecting the market from potential risks associated with these advanced trading strategies.

The regulatory landscape for High-Frequency Trading continues to evolve as authorities aim to adapt to technological advancements while maintaining market integrity. Measures like the Volcker Rule, by restricting banks' speculative investments, have implications for the liquidity and nature of HFT activities. The Tick Size Pilot Program was an initiative to test whether larger tick sizes would benefit the market quality for smaller capitalization stocks, a move that could affect HFT profitability and strategies. These regulations, among others, represent ongoing efforts to balance the benefits of HFT, like liquidity and efficiency, with potential risks such as market volatility and systemic issues. The future of HFT regulation will likely continue to be a dynamic interplay between innovation in trading technologies and the safeguarding of market fairness and stability.

With advances in artificial intelligence and machine learning, the face of HFT is changing, becoming more adaptive and intelligent. The arms race for speed may be reaching its physical limits, but the strategies continue to evolve, presenting new challenges and opportunities for traders and regulators alike.

The future of High-Frequency Trading (HFT) lies in the intersection of advanced computing, data analysis, and financial theory. With the potential physical limits of speed being approached, the focus may shift more towards strategic and intelligent algorithms, incorporating elements of artificial intelligence and machine learning. These technologies could enable more adaptive, predictive trading strategies, possibly making the HFT landscape even more competitive.

Environmental, social, and governance (ESG) factors are increasingly becoming part of the trading conversation, suggesting that HFT strategies may also evolve to integrate these aspects into their algorithms. This progression points towards a more complex, multifaceted future for HFT, where technology, strategy, and ethics converge in the pursuit of market efficiency and profitability.

Pseudocode for a Simple High-Frequency Trading Algorithm

```
# Define trading parameters
threshold = 0.01 # Price change threshold to trigger a trade
volume = 100 # Number of shares to trade

# Monitor the order book
order_book = get_order_book('Stock_Ticker')

# Trading logic
while True:
    best_bid = order_book.get_best_bid()
    best_ask = order_book.get_best_ask()

    if best_ask['price'] - best_bid['price'] <= threshold:
        # If the spread is less than or equal to the threshold, execute trades
        place_order(buy, 'Stock_Ticker', price=best_ask['price'], volume=volume)
        place_order(sell, 'Stock_Ticker', price=best_bid['price'], volume=volume)

    # Update the order book
    order_book.update()
```

```
# Pseudocode for a Simple High-Frequency Trading Algorithm

# Define trading parameters
threshold = 0.01  # Price change threshold to trigger a trade
volume = 100  # Number of shares to trade

# Monitor the order book
order_book = get_order_book('Stock_Ticker')

# Trading logic
while True:
    best_bid = order_book.get_best_bid()
    best_ask = order_book.get_best_ask()

    if best_ask['price'] - best_bid['price'] <= threshold:
        # If the spread is less than or equal to the threshold, execute trades
        place_order(buy, 'Stock_Ticker', price=best_ask['price'], volume=volume)
        place_order(sell, 'Stock_Ticker', price=best_bid['price'], volume=volume)

    # Update the order book
    order_book.update()
```

Predictive Analytics

Predictive analytics in quantitative trading leverages big data and machine learning (ML) to forecast market movements. These algorithms sift through vast and diverse datasets – including price movements, economic indicators, and social media sentiments – to detect patterns and insights beyond human analysis.

Machine learning models like neural networks, decision trees, and support vector machines are trained on historical data to predict future market trends. They can identify subtle correlations and causal relationships that are not apparent through traditional analysis.

Deep learning, a subset of ML, is particularly potent in predictive analytics. Neural networks with multiple layers can process and interpret complex data structures, making them ideal for financial markets characterized by non-linear relationships and high volatility.

Predictive models are continuously refined with new data, adapting to market changes. However, the complexity of these models and the opaqueness of their decision-making processes can be challenging, necessitating careful management and regular oversight to ensure accuracy and mitigate risk.

The complexities of predictive analytics in quantitative trading, particularly when involving big data and machine learning, continue to be a significant focus for traders and financial analysts. The algorithms used for this purpose are designed to handle large volumes of data from diverse sources. This includes not just market data but also alternative data sources like social media, economic reports, and geopolitical events.

These algorithms apply advanced techniques, including natural language processing to interpret news and sentiment analysis to gauge market mood.

One of the critical challenges in predictive analytics is the accurate processing and interpretation of this data. Techniques like feature engineering are used to identify which aspects of the data are most predictive of market movements. The models must also be robust enough to adapt to changing market conditions, a process known as model retraining.

Moreover, the application of deep learning, particularly recurrent neural networks (RNNs) and long short-term memory networks (LSTMs), has enhanced the ability to analyze time-series data. These models are capable of understanding complex temporal dynamics and are instrumental in forecasting price movements.

Another advanced approach involves reinforcement learning, where algorithms learn optimal trading strategies by interacting with a simulated market environment. This method allows algorithms to learn from their actions, continuously improving their decision-making process.

However, these advanced methods come with their own set of challenges. Overfitting remains a significant concern, where models perform well on historical data but fail to generalize to new, unseen data. Ensuring model transparency and interpretability is also crucial, especially in a highly regulated industry like finance.

The use of predictive analytics in quantitative trading represents a blend of financial expertise, statistical theory, and advanced computing. While these tools offer powerful capabilities for market prediction, they also require careful management and continuous refinement to ensure they remain effective and aligned with market realities.

CHAPTER 11: CASE STUDIES AND LESSONS FROM SUCCESSFUL ALGORITHMIC

TRADERS

Case Study: Renaissance Technologies and Jim Simons

In this section, we will explore the success story of Renaissance Technologies, a world-renowned quantitative hedge fund, and its founder, Jim Simons. By examining the techniques, strategies, and philosophies behind the firm's success, we can glean valuable insights into the world of algorithmic trading and draw lessons that can be applied to our own trading ventures.

Background

Renaissance Technologies was founded in 1982 by Jim Simons, a former mathematician and codebreaker. Today, the firm is widely regarded as one of the most successful quantitative hedge funds in the world, with its flagship Medallion Fund generating astonishing annual returns for more than three decades. By harnessing the power of advanced mathematical models, Renaissance Technologies has consistently outperformed its peers and become a pioneer in the field of quantitative finance.

Jim Simons' background in mathematics and cryptography laid the foundation for the firm's approach to algorithmic trading. His academic career played a significant role in shaping the investment approach at Renaissance Technologies. He earned his Ph.D. in mathematics from the University of California, Berkeley, and later worked as a codebreaker for the United States National Security Agency (NSA) and as a mathematics professor at Stony Brook University.

Renaissance Technologies is known for its flagship fund, the Medallion Fund, which has consistently delivered exceptional returns since its inception in 1988. The Medallion Fund employs a highly secretive quantitative trading strategy, using complex mathematical models and algorithms to identify and exploit patterns in financial markets. It is primarily focused on short-term trading and has been extremely successful due to its ability to consistently generate high returns with low correlation to traditional investment markets.

As a result of the firm's success and the exceptional performance of the Medallion Fund, Jim Simons is often referred to as one of the greatest investors on Wall Street and the most successful hedge fund manager of all time. In addition to his work at Renaissance Technologies, Simons is also a noted philanthropist, supporting various initiatives in science, education, and health through his foundation, the Simons Foundation

The Medallion Fund

The Medallion Fund is the flagship fund of Renaissance Technologies and is considered one of the most successful hedge funds of all time. The fund has generated an average annual return of over 35% since its inception, even after accounting for high management and performance fees. This level of performance is unrivaled in the industry and serves as a testament to the power of algorithmic trading and quantitative analysis.

Renaissance Strategies and Techniques

Renaissance Technologies employs a diverse range of trading strategies and techniques in its pursuit of market-beating returns. Some of the key aspects of the firm's approach include:

1. Data-driven decision-making: The firm's success is largely attributed to its ability to process vast amounts of data and uncover hidden patterns and relationships within the data. By leveraging advanced statistical models and machine learning techniques, Renaissance Technologies can identify profitable trading opportunities that may be overlooked by traditional investors.

2. Diversification: Renaissance Technologies' trading strategies are highly diversified, with the firm trading a wide range of asset classes, including equities, fixed income, currencies, and commodities. This diversification helps to spread risk and reduce the potential impact of adverse market events on the firm's overall performance.

3. Short-term trading: The firm primarily focuses on short-term trading opportunities, with many of its strategies holding positions for just a few days or even hours. This approach allows the firm to capitalize on small market inefficiencies and reduce the impact of external factors, such as macroeconomic events or changes in market sentiment.

4. Continuous improvement: Renaissance Technologies places a strong emphasis on continuous research and improvement of its trading strategies. The firm

employs a team of highly skilled researchers, including mathematicians, physicists, and computer scientists, who are tasked with developing new models and refining existing ones.

Lessons from Renaissance Technologies and Jim Simons

While the success of Renaissance Technologies and Jim Simons may seem unattainable for most individual traders, there are several key lessons that can be applied to our own trading endeavors:

1. Embrace technology and quantitative methods: The success of Renaissance Technologies highlights the potential of algorithmic trading and quantitative analysis in generating superior investment returns. By embracing technology and advanced mathematical techniques, traders can uncover profitable trading opportunities that may be inaccessible through traditional methods.

2. Focus on data quality and data-driven decision-making: The importance of reliable and diverse data sources cannot be overstated. Traders should prioritize the acquisition, cleaning, and processing of high-quality data to ensure the accuracy of their trading models and the effectiveness of their decision-making processes.

3. Diversify your trading strategies: Diversification is not only important for managing risk but also for improving the performance of your trading portfolio. By employing a diverse range of trading strategies and techniques, traders can increase their chances of capturing market inefficiencies and achieving consistent returns.

4. Adapt and evolve: The world of finance is constantly

changing, and traders must be willing to adapt and evolve their strategies in response to shifting market conditions. Continuous research and improvement are essential for maintaining a competitive edge and staying ahead of the curve.

5. Build a strong team: The success of Renaissance Technologies can be partially attributed to the firm's talented and diverse team of researchers and traders. By surrounding yourself with skilled professionals and fostering a culture of collaboration, you can increase the likelihood of achieving success in the world of algorithmic trading.

The story of Renaissance Technologies and Jim Simons serves as a powerful reminder of the potential of algorithmic trading and quantitative analysis. By embracing advanced mathematical techniques, harnessing the power of technology, and adopting a disciplined approach to trading, it is possible to achieve remarkable success in the world of finance.

Case Study: D.E. Shaw & Co. and David E. Shaw

In this section, we will delve into the success story of D.E. Shaw & Co., a leading global investment firm, and its founder, David E. Shaw. By examining the strategies, techniques, and philosophies that have contributed to the company's achievements, we can gain valuable insights into the world of algorithmic trading and apply these lessons to our own trading ventures.

D.E. Shaw Group Background

D.E. Shaw & Co. was founded in 1988 by David E. Shaw, a former computer scientist who had worked at Columbia University and Morgan Stanley. The company has grown to become one of the largest and most successful hedge funds in the world, with billions of dollars in assets under management. D.E. Shaw & Co. is widely recognized for its pioneering work in quantitative finance and algorithmic trading, which has played a significant role in the firm's long-term success.

David E. Shaw's background in computer science laid the groundwork for the company's innovative approach to investment management. By harnessing the power of advanced computational models and sophisticated algorithms, D.E. Shaw & Co. has consistently outperformed its peers and cemented its reputation as a leader in the field of quantitative finance.

The D.E. Shaw Group manages a variety of investment funds, each with a distinct investment focus and strategy. Some of the company's flagship funds include the D.E. Shaw Composite Fund and the D.E. Shaw Oculus Fund, both of which have generated impressive returns over the years. The firm's ability to offer a diverse range of investment strategies has contributed to its enduring success and allowed it to attract a wide array of institutional and individual investors.

D.E. Shaw Group Strategies and Techniques

D.E. Shaw & Co. employs a diverse range of trading strategies and techniques in its quest for market-beating returns. Some of the key aspects of the company's approach include:

1. Data-driven decision-making: The firm's success can be largely attributed to its ability to process and analyze vast amounts of data, uncovering hidden patterns and relationships within the data. By leveraging advanced statistical models and machine learning techniques, D.E. Shaw & Co. can identify profitable trading opportunities that might be overlooked by traditional investors.

2. Diversification: The company's trading strategies are highly diversified, spanning a wide range of asset classes, including equities, fixed income, currencies, and commodities. This diversification helps to spread risk and reduce the potential impact of adverse market events on the firm's overall performance.

3. Systematic approach: D.E. Shaw & Co. is known for its systematic approach to trading, which relies on algorithms and computational models rather than human discretion. This approach allows the firm to maintain a high level of discipline and consistency in its trading activities, reducing the potential for human error and emotion-driven decision-making.

4. Continuous improvement: The firm places a strong emphasis on continuous research and improvement of its trading strategies. D.E. Shaw & Co. employs a team of highly skilled researchers, including mathematicians, physicists, and computer scientists, who are tasked with developing new models and refining existing ones.

Lessons from D.E. Shaw & Co. and David E. Shaw

The success of D.E. Shaw & Co. and its founder, David E. Shaw, offers valuable lessons that can be applied to our own trading endeavors:

1. Embrace technology and quantitative methods: The achievements of D.E. Shaw & Co. underscore the potential of algorithmic trading and quantitative analysis in generating superior investment returns. By embracing technology and advanced mathematical techniques, traders can uncover profitable trading opportunities that may be inaccessible through traditional methods.

2. Diversify your strategies: The diverse range of trading strategies employed by D.E. Shaw & Co. highlights the importance of diversification in achieving long-term success. By spreading risk across various asset classes and trading techniques, investors can reduce the potential impact of market volatility and increase their chances of consistent returns.

3. Focus on data-driven decision-making: Like Renaissance Technologies, D.E. Shaw & Co. relies heavily on data-driven decision-making to identify profitable trading opportunities. By developing a deep understanding of market data and employing advanced statistical techniques, traders can improve their ability to make informed investment decisions.

4. Maintain a systematic approach: The systematic approach employed by D.E. Shaw & Co. emphasizes the importance of discipline and consistency in trading. By relying on algorithms and computational models rather than human discretion, traders can reduce the potential for emotional decision-making and human error, which can undermine long-term success.

5. Prioritize continuous improvement: D.E. Shaw & Co.'s commitment to continuous research and improvement demonstrates the importance of staying ahead of the curve in the ever-evolving world of finance. By dedicating resources to ongoing research and development, traders can ensure that their strategies remain relevant and competitive in the face of changing market conditions.

The story of D.E. Shaw & Co. and David E. Shaw serves as an inspiring example of the power of technology, quantitative methods, and systematic trading in the world of finance. By embracing these principles and focusing on data-driven decision-making, diversification, and continuous improvement, traders can increase their chances of success and pave the way for a prosperous future in algorithmic trading.

Case Studies: Two Sigma and Citadel

In this section, we will explore the success stories of two leading quantitative hedge funds, Two Sigma and Citadel, as well as a brief overview of other notable quantitative hedge funds and traders. By examining their strategies, techniques, and philosophies, we can gain valuable insights that can be applied to our own algorithmic trading ventures.

Two Sigma Background

Two Sigma was founded in 2001 by David Siegel, a computer scientist, and John Overdeck, a former managing director at D.E. Shaw & Co. The firm is headquartered in New York and has rapidly grown to become one of the world's largest and most successful quantitative hedge funds, with billions of dollars in assets under management. Two Sigma's success is primarily attributed to its innovative use of technology and data-driven investment strategies.

Two Sigma Strategies and Techniques:

Two Sigma employs a diverse range of trading strategies and techniques, focusing on data-driven decision-making and advanced computational models. Some key aspects of the firm's approach include:

Emphasis on artificial intelligence and machine learning: Two Sigma leverages advanced AI and machine learning techniques to uncover patterns and relationships within vast amounts of data, allowing the firm to identify unique investment opportunities.
Diversification across asset classes: The firm employs a multi-strategy approach, investing in various asset classes, including

equities, fixed income, currencies, and commodities.

Systematic trading: Two Sigma relies on systematic trading strategies, using algorithms and computational models to make investment decisions, thereby reducing the potential for human error and emotion-driven decision-making.

Citadel Background

Citadel was founded in 1990 by Kenneth Griffin, a former trader at Credit Suisse First Boston. Based in Chicago, Citadel has grown to become one of the largest and most successful hedge funds in the world, with billions of dollars in assets under management. Citadel is renowned for its sophisticated trading strategies and cutting-edge technology.

Citadel Strategies and Techniques:

Citadel employs a wide range of trading strategies and techniques, including:

- High-frequency trading (HFT): Citadel is known for its expertise in HFT, which involves the rapid execution of trades using sophisticated algorithms and high-speed data networks.
- Market-making and arbitrage: The firm engages in market-making activities, providing liquidity to financial markets, and seeks to profit from arbitrage opportunities that arise from pricing inefficiencies.
- Diversification across asset classes: Like Two Sigma and D.E. Shaw & Co., Citadel invests in various asset classes, including equities, fixed income, currencies, and commodities.

Other Notable Quantitative Hedge Funds and Traders

In addition to Two Sigma and Citadel, several other hedge funds and traders have achieved success in the world of quantitative finance:

- AQR Capital Management:
Founded by Cliff Asness and several other partners, AQR Capital Management is known for its quantitative investment strategies and focus on academic research.

- Bridgewater Associates:
Founded by Ray Dalio, Bridgewater Associates is one of the largest hedge funds in the world and employs a systematic, data-driven approach to investment management.

- Winton Group:
Founded by David Harding, Winton Group is a leading quantitative investment management firm that utilizes scientific research and advanced technology to develop its trading strategies.

Lessons from Two Sigma, Citadel, and Other Quantitative Hedge Funds and Traders

The success of quantitative hedge funds and traders like Two Sigma, Citadel, and others offers valuable lessons that can be applied to our own trading endeavors:

- Embrace technology and quantitative methods: The achievements of these firms underscore the potential of algorithmic trading and quantitative analysis in generating superior investment returns. By embracing technology and quantitative methods, traders can uncover unique opportunities and improve their decision-making processes.

- Diversify across asset classes and strategies: The multi-strategy approach employed by these firms demonstrates the importance of diversification in managing risk and achieving consistent returns. By investing in various asset classes and employing a range of trading techniques, traders can mitigate the impact of market volatility and increase their chances of success.

- Focus on data-driven decision-making: The success of these firms is largely attributed to their reliance on data-driven decision-making. By developing a deep understanding of market data and employing advanced statistical techniques, traders can enhance their ability to make informed investment decisions.

- Maintain a systematic approach: The systematic approach employed by these firms emphasizes the importance of discipline and consistency in trading. By relying on algorithms and computational models rather than human discretion, traders can reduce the potential for emotional decision-making and human error, which can undermine long-term success.

- Prioritize continuous improvement: The commitment to ongoing research and development exhibited by these firms highlights the importance of staying ahead of the curve in the ever-evolving world of finance. By dedicating resources to continuous research and improvement, traders can ensure that their strategies remain relevant and competitive in the face of changing market conditions.

The success of Two Sigma, Citadel, and other quantitative hedge funds and traders serves as a powerful testament to the potential of algorithmic trading and quantitative finance. By embracing technology, data-driven decision-making, diversification, and a systematic approach, traders can increase their chances of success in the financial markets.

CONCLUSION

As we reach the end of our comprehensive guide to algorithmic trading, it is essential to reflect on the key principles, methodologies, and insights that have been presented throughout the book. Algorithmic trading is a complex and highly competitive field that requires a combination of quantitative skills, technology prowess, and an understanding of financial markets. By leveraging the knowledge and techniques discussed in this guide, aspiring traders can develop a solid foundation for building a successful algorithmic trading business.

In this conclusion, we will summarize the critical aspects of algorithmic trading covered in the guide and provide some final thoughts on the future of the industry.

Algorithmic trading involves the use of computer algorithms to execute trades in financial markets automatically. This approach offers several advantages over traditional manual trading, including increased speed, reduced trading costs, and the ability to process large volumes of data. Algorithmic trading has become increasingly popular in recent years, with a growing number of market participants adopting these methods to improve their trading outcomes.

Effective data management is crucial for the success of any algorithmic trading business. Traders need to have access to reliable and diverse data sources, including market data, fundamental data, and alternative data, to develop and implement profitable trading strategies. Proper data handling, including data cleaning, preprocessing, and storage, is essential for ensuring the integrity and accuracy of the data used in the decision-making process.

Quantitative analysis and modeling techniques form the backbone of algorithmic trading strategies. By employing statistical methods, machine learning algorithms, and optimization techniques, traders can identify patterns and relationships within the data, develop predictive models, and optimize their trading strategies to maximize returns while minimizing risk.

Developing and backtesting trading algorithms is a critical step in the algorithmic trading process. Traders must rigorously test their strategies using historical data to ensure their effectiveness and robustness in different market conditions. Proper backtesting can help identify potential issues and improve the overall performance of the trading strategy.

Effective execution and order management are vital components of successful algorithmic trading. Traders must carefully consider factors such as liquidity, market impact, and transaction costs when executing trades. By employing advanced order types and routing strategies, traders can minimize adverse effects and achieve optimal trade execution.

Investing in the right infrastructure and technology is essential for the success of an algorithmic trading business. This includes hardware and networking requirements, software and programming languages, and the selection of appropriate APIs and trading platforms. By leveraging cutting-edge technology, traders can increase the efficiency and performance of their trading strategies.

Algorithmic traders must navigate a complex regulatory landscape and ensure compliance with various rules and regulations. This includes adhering to best execution practices, managing risk, and maintaining proper recordkeeping. By staying informed about regulatory changes and implementing robust compliance measures, traders can mitigate potential risks and protect their business.

Achieving long-term success in algorithmic trading requires more than just technical knowledge and skill. Traders must develop a competitive edge, protect their intellectual property, manage talent, and continuously research and improve their strategies. By focusing on these critical aspects and maintaining a disciplined approach, traders can build a thriving algorithmic trading business that generates consistent returns.

As financial markets continue to evolve, algorithmic trading is poised to play an increasingly significant role. Advances in technology, data science, and machine learning will drive further innovation in trading strategies and techniques. Traders who embrace these advancements and stay ahead of the curve will be well-positioned to succeed in the competitive world of algorithmic trading.

REFERENCES

In this section, we will provide a comprehensive list of books, articles, websites, reports, and studies that can serve as valuable references for those interested in learning more about algorithmic trading and quantitative finance.

Books

1. "Algorithmic Trading: Winning Strategies and Their Rationale" by Ernest P. Chan
2. "Inside the Black Box: A Simple Guide to Quantitative and High-Frequency Trading" by Rishi K. Narang
3. "Quantitative Trading: How to Build Your Own Algorithmic Trading Business" by Ernie Chan
4. "Trading Systems: A New Approach to System Development and Portfolio Optimisation" by Emilio Tomasini and Urban Jaekle
5. "The Quants: How a New Breed of Math Whizzes Conquered Wall Street and Nearly Destroyed It" by Scott Patterson
6. "The Alchemy of Finance: Reading the Mind of the Market" by George Soros
7. "Market Wizards: Interviews with Top Traders" by Jack D. Schwager
8. "Flash Boys: A Wall Street Revolt" by Michael Lewis
9. "Dark Pools: The Rise of the Machine Traders and the Rigging of the U.S. Stock Market" by Scott Patterson
10. "A Man for All Markets: From Las Vegas to Wall Street, How I Beat the Dealer and the Market" by Edward O.

Thorp

Articles

1) "The World's Most Successful Hedge Fund Manager" by Gregory Zuckerman, The Wall Street Journal
2) "Inside the Secret World of Quantitative Trading" by Matthew Philips, Bloomberg Businessweek
3) "How Renaissance's Medallion Fund Became Finance's Blackest Box" by Katherine Burton, Bloomberg
4) "The Rise of the Artificially Intelligent Hedge Fund" by Cade Metz, WIRED
5) "The Quants Run Wall Street Now" by Gregory Zuckerman and Bradley Hope, The Wall Street Journal
6) "Algos, Barriers, and the Future of Trading" by Robert Iati, The Trade
7) "A Brief History of High-Frequency Trading" by Erik Spanberg, Institutional Investor

Websites

1. Quantopian (www.quantopian.com): A platform for developing, testing, and executing algorithmic trading strategies.
2. QuantConnect (www.quantconnect.com): An online platform for building and testing algorithmic trading strategies.
3. Quantocracy (www.quantocracy.com): A curated collection of articles and research on quantitative trading and finance.
4. QuantStart (www.quantstart.com): An educational resource for learning about quantitative finance, trading, and programming.
5. QuantInsti (www.quantinsti.com): A provider of online courses and certifications in algorithmic trading and quantitative finance.

Reports and Studies

1. "The Role of High-Frequency Trading in Modern Markets" by Terrence Hendershott, Charles M. Jones, and Albert J. Menkveld
2. "High-Frequency Trading and Price Discovery" by Jonathan Brogaard, Terrence Hendershott, and Ryan Riordan
3. "The Flash Crash: The Impact of High-Frequency Trading on an Electronic Market" by Andrei Kirilenko, Albert S. Kyle, Mehrdad Samadi, and Tugkan Tuzun
4. "Evaluating the Performance of the Lee-Ready Trade Classification Algorithm" by Robert P. Bartlett III and Justin McCrary
5. "The Impact of Algorithmic Trading on Market Liquidity: Evidence from the Canadian Market" by Katya Malinova and Andreas Park
6. "Institutional Adoption of Algorithmic Trading: A Case Study" by Gomber, Peter, and Markus Gsell
7. "Algorithmic Trading Patterns in Xetra Orders" by Gideon Saar, Rosario Russo, and Michael Riordan
8. "The Future of Computer Trading in Financial Markets: An International Perspective" by Foresight, UK Government Office for Science
9. "A Dynamic Model of High-Frequency Trading" by John D. Farmer and Spyros Skouras
10. "The Impact of Algorithmic Trading on Market Quality: Evidence from the European Union" by Marco Pagano and Alireza Tahbaz-Salehi

Academic Journals

1. Journal of Trading (www.iijournals.com/JOT): A publication focusing on the practice and implementation of trading strategies, technology, and

regulation.
2. Journal of Financial Markets (www.journals.elsevier.com/journal-of-financial-markets): A journal covering topics related to market microstructure, trading, and financial markets in general.
3. Journal of Empirical Finance (www.journals.elsevier.com/journal-of-empirical-finance): A journal dedicated to the publication of empirical research in finance, including studies on algorithmic trading and market microstructure.
4. Quantitative Finance (www.tandfonline.com/toc/rquf20/current): A journal focusing on the interdisciplinary field of quantitative finance, including studies on algorithmic trading, risk management, and financial engineering.

These resources provide a wealth of information on algorithmic trading, quantitative finance, and related topics. By leveraging these references, readers can gain a deeper understanding of the field and its various nuances, ultimately enhancing their own trading strategies and methodologies.

ACKNOWLEDGEMENT

Penning this book has been both an enlightening journey and a challenging endeavor. Along the way, a multitude of individuals have provided unwavering support, guidance, and inspiration, and it's with immense gratitude that I wish to recognize their contributions.

Firstly, I'd like to extend my heartfelt appreciation to my family, whose constant encouragement and belief in my vision provided the impetus to bring this work to fruition. To my dear partner, your patience and understanding during the countless hours spent writing have been the bedrock upon which this book stands.

Special thanks to my team at Other People's Capital. The collective brilliance and dedication you all bring to our ventures served as a continual source of inspiration for the insights shared in these pages.

I'm deeply indebted to my colleagues and mentors from the financial industry. Your vast reservoirs of knowledge and experiences have shaped my understanding of scalability in business, enriching the content of this book.

To my editorial team, led by Lisa Green and Mark Roberts, thank you for painstakingly sifting through drafts, refining ideas, and ensuring that the narrative retained clarity while capturing the essence of the subject. Your dedication to excellence is palpable on every page.

A special nod to the countless guests and listeners of "Innovate

Now: The Pulse of Future Technologies." Your insights, questions, and feedback have, time and again, driven home the importance of the topic at hand and have sparked many of the ideas discussed in this book.

Lastly, to you, dear reader. Your quest for knowledge, your dedication to your enterprise, and your belief in the potential of scalability are the very reasons this book exists. My deepest hope is that the insights shared herein empower you in your journey toward sustained growth and success.

Every page of this book carries the imprints of all of you. From the depths of my heart, thank you.

ABOUT THE AUTHOR

Josh Luberisse

Josh, a multifaceted entrepreneur and renowned author, has carved a niche for himself in the spheres of artificial intelligence, geopolitics, finance, and cybersecurity. With a myriad of authoritative books to his credit on these subjects, he is undeniably a luminary in the domain. Not just an author, Josh is also the charismatic host of "Innovate Now: The Pulse of Future Technologies," a groundbreaking podcast that unravels the intricacies of nascent technologies and the imminent future of innovation, accentuating on avant-garde progressions in AI, fintech, and quantum computing.

His eclectic professional journey is an embodiment of diverse experiences. From serving at financial behemoths like Citi, Bank of America, BNY Mellon, Morgan Stanley, to JP Morgan Chase, his immersion in the financial industry is profound. His multilateral expertise as a licensed real estate agent, tax advisor, and a sagacious planner for retirement and estates accentuates the depth and breadth of his knowledge, enabling him to write with an unparalleled, informed perspective. This ensures that his readers are always at the forefront of understanding and action.

However, it's not just the financial world that has witnessed

Josh's Midas touch. As an astute entrepreneur, Josh has birthed and nurtured several startups. His brainchild, Neuromorph Systems, stands as a testament to his vision. A future global tech titan, it specializes in data management, system integration, and artificial intelligence. With a mission to shield the pivotal systems of its global clientele and concurrently offer them unparalleled data management, visualization, and analysis capabilities, Neuromorph Systems remains a beacon in sectors as diverse as government, entertainment, transportation, and finance, to name a few.

In the realm of venture capital, Josh's VC firm, Other People's Capital, emerges as a game-changer. Dedicated to bolstering founders with groundbreaking ideas, the company's expertise lies in fostering and propelling enterprises that have the potential to define entire categories. With a track record replete with highly successful exits, Other People's Capital has a legacy of identifying and nurturing businesses that ascend to industry leadership.

Furthermore, with OptimalOrbit, Josh aspires to metamorphose the logistics industry. By leveraging state-of-the-art technologies, he envisions bridging the chasm between shippers, carriers, and the digital dimension. With its core mission being the facilitation of seamless operations and sustainable growth for clients, OptimalOrbit is a harbinger of enhanced efficiency and cost optimization in logistics. Through the implementation of disruptive technologies such as AI, blockchain, and machine learning, OptimalOrbit's avant-garde algorithms are poised to reshape the logistics landscape, offering clients unparalleled business process optimization.

Josh's journey, from his stint in the financial realm to his foray into the world of startups, underlines his unmatched expertise and vision. As a thought leader, seasoned practitioner, and an indomitable entrepreneur, his writings and ventures are not just about envisioning the future but also about shaping it.

BOOKS IN THIS SERIES

Business & Finance

From Calamity To Stability: Harnessing The Wisdom Of Past Financial Crises To Build A Stable And Resilient Global Financial System

In 'From Calamity to Stability: Harnessing the Wisdom of Past Financial Crises to Build a Stable and Resilient Global Financial System', author Josh delves deep into the history of financial crises, examining the causes, impacts, and lessons learned from each event. With a keen analytical approach, Josh expertly navigates the complex landscape of financial regulation, supervision, and policy that has evolved in response to these crises.

Drawing on a wealth of research and firsthand experience, the book presents a comprehensive overview of the regulatory frameworks that have emerged over time, from the Glass-Steagall Act to the Dodd-Frank Wall Street Reform and Consumer Protection Act, as well as the development of international standards such as the Basel Accords. By analyzing the interplay between innovation and stability, Josh identifies key areas where further action is necessary to maintain a resilient financial system capable of supporting sustainable economic growth.

Through a careful examination of the role of international

cooperation, transparency, and trust in fostering financial stability, 'From Calamity to Stability' offers valuable insights into the challenges and opportunities facing policymakers, financial institutions, and society at large. The book not only underscores the importance of learning from past financial crises but also highlights the need for a flexible, forward-looking regulatory framework that can adapt to emerging trends and challenges.

'From Calamity to Stability' is an essential resource for anyone seeking to understand the complex dynamics of the global financial system and the ongoing efforts to ensure its stability and resilience. With its balanced and informed perspective, this book provides a compelling roadmap for navigating the uncertain global economic landscape and building a more secure financial future for all.

The New Profit Paradigm: Balancing Shareholder Value With Stakeholder Engagement

Our existing economic infrastructure is under strain. We stand at a turning point where we can reshape it into a system that fosters prosperity for all stakeholders, prioritizing sustainability, and holistic success. To do so, we must address several pressing issues. First, it is imperative to confront the stagnation of wage growth amid rising income disparity. Second, we need to check the disproportionate market power that large corporations exercise, which stifles innovation and restricts productivity.

Josh draws on his extensive experience in the corporate world to offer a fresh perspective in "The New Profit Paradigm: Balancing Shareholder Value with Stakeholder Engagement". He argues that to truly tackle these challenges, we must first recognize and understand the issues in our current economic framework.

In his meticulously crafted work, Josh investigates successful practices from across the globe, offering valuable insights into the real-world application of stakeholder capitalism. Throughout the book, he reveals innovative strategies and approaches that promise a more balanced and equitable future, including:

- The Rise of Stakeholder Capitalism: Understanding the shift and how it challenges the traditional business model
- Balancing Stakeholder Interests: Who are the key stakeholders and why their interests matter?
- Building Trust with Stakeholders: The critical role of transparency and open communication
- Engaging Employees as Stakeholders: Addressing the demand for meaningful work and flexibility

With a clear-eyed view of our economic reality, "The New Profit Paradigm: Balancing Shareholder Value with Stakeholder Engagement" provides actionable pathways to face our challenges. Throughout the book, Josh illustrates how everyone - from governments to corporations to individuals - can take steps to revitalize the fragments of our global economy, creating a system that ultimately benefits all stakeholders.

The Ultimate Guide To Us Financial Regulations: A Primer For Lawyers And Business Professionals

Over the past several decades, the financial landscape and its regulation have experienced unprecedented growth and transformation. This era has seen significant advancements in financial markets, along with cyclical periods of regulatory reform, often in response to crisis situations. The recent financial crisis has generated immense interest in financial regulation from policymakers, economists, legal practitioners, and academics alike, sparking comprehensive regulatory reforms.

The Ultimate Guide to US Financial Regulations: A Primer for Lawyers and Business Professionals delivers an authoritative, up-to-date, and in-depth examination of the intricacies of financial regulation. With insights on banking, securities, derivatives, insurance, consumer financial protection, anti-money laundering, and international financial regulations, this comprehensive guide employs a contextual and comparative approach to explore academic, policy, and regulatory requirements.

The initial sections of the guide delve into the foundational themes that underpin financial regulation: financial systems and their regulation; the structure of financial system regulation; the evolution of Financial Regulation; the role of regulatory agencies as well as their various enforcement mechanisms; as well as insurance, banking and securities regulations. The latter sections focus on the core objectives of financial regulation, and explore key topics such as deposit insurance, consumer protection regulations, safety and soundness requirements, insider trading, securities fraud, and investment advisor regulations. The Ultimate Guide to US Financial Regulations offers an indispensable resource for understanding and navigating the complex world of financial regulation, making it an essential read for professionals across the legal and business spectrum.

The Insider's Guide To Securities Law: Navigating The Intricacies Of Public And Private Offerings

Navigate the intricate world of private equity and venture capital with "The Insider's Guide to Securities Law: Navigating the Intricacies of Public and Private Offerings." This comprehensive guidebook illuminates the complexities of the industry, serving as an essential resource for legal practitioners, investment professionals, and entrepreneurs alike.

Venture into the fascinating domain of fund formation, understand the roles of limited and general partners, and uncover the strategic aspects of tax structuring. Get acquainted with the key regulatory authorities overseeing the industry, including the Securities and Exchange Commission (SEC), the Financial Industry Regulatory Authority (FINRA), and the Commodity Futures Trading Commission (CFTC).

Delve deeper into the regulatory landscape, exploring crucial compliance requirements, the essentialities of fiduciary duty, and the impact of the JOBS Act and other significant laws. Grasp the essentials of Anti-Money Laundering (AML) and Know Your Customer (KYC) compliance, and learn how to navigate through the processes of sourcing and closing deals, conducting due diligence, and managing and exiting investments effectively.

"The Insider's Guide to Securities Law" offers practical insights, actionable strategies, and a detailed glossary of key terms, making the labyrinth of private equity and venture capital law accessible to both seasoned professionals and newcomers. Embark on a journey through the dynamic landscape of global finance with confidence and insight with this indispensable guide.

Acing Your Sie Exam: An In-Depth Guide To Securities Industry Essentials

Master the world of securities and set yourself up for success in the financial industry with 'Acing Your SIE Exam: An In-Depth Guide to the Securities Industry Essentials' This in-depth guide is designed to equip aspiring securities professionals with the knowledge and strategies they need to pass the SIE exam, an essential stepping stone towards a rewarding career in the securities industry.

Carefully aligned with the content of the SIE exam, this guide covers a wide array of topics: from understanding the intricacies of market structure and the functions of regulatory agencies, to detailed insights into equity and debt securities, options, investment companies, and more. It provides thorough explanations of trading procedures, customer account management, and important legislation that shapes the industry.

Beyond the raw information, this guide also aids in mastering the art of exam-taking. It offers invaluable advice on how to study effectively, manage your time, and develop successful test-taking strategies. The book's clear, easy-to-understand language makes complex concepts approachable, irrespective of your background in finance.

To enhance your understanding, each chapter is coupled with practical examples and key takeaways. Also included is a comprehensive glossary that provides clear definitions of the key terms you'll encounter on the exam.

"Acing Your SIE Exam: An In-Depth Guide to the Securities Industry Essentials" is more than just a study guide. It's a resource designed to launch your securities career. With this guide in your hands, you are well on your way to acing the SIE exam and establishing a strong foundation for your future in the financial industry.

Private Equity Demystified: A Comprehensive Guide For Investors, Finance Professionals And Business School Students

Discover the secrets of the private equity industry and learn how to navigate the complex world of investments with "Private Equity Demystified: A Comprehensive Guide for Investors, Finance Professionals and Business School Students". This book is a must-read for anyone looking to understand the inner workings of private equity, from the different types of funds and strategies, to the importance of due diligence and exit strategies. It also explores the role of private equity in emerging markets and the future of the industry.

With real-life case studies and insights from industry leaders and experts, this book will give you the tools and knowledge you need to make informed investment decisions and pursue a successful career in private equity. So, whether you're an aspiring finance professional, an experienced investor, or business school students looking to expand their knowledge of private equity this book is the essential resource to better understand the world of private equity.

BOOKS BY THIS AUTHOR

Silent Wars: Espionage, Sabotage, And The Covert Battles In Cyberspace

Silent Wars: Espionage, Sabotage, and the Covert Battles in Cyberspace delves into the shadowy world of covert cyber conflict, that unfold beyond the public eye. Scrutinizing the intricate balance between espionage and assault, the author, Josh, disentangles the convoluted web of digital warfare, where the line between intelligence-gathering and outright attack blurs.

Silent Wars navigates the intricate landscape of covert cyber operations, examining a multitude of cases that shed light on the diverse tactics and strategies employed by nations in this modern arena of intangible warfare. Through a meticulous analysis of case studies, military doctrines, and technical underpinnings, Josh unveils the striking reality that contemporary cyber operations, while seemingly groundbreaking, still embody the age-old essence of conflict waged through non-physical domains such as information space and the electromagnetic spectrum.

Silent Wars breaks down the multifaceted nature of offensive cyber operations, emphasizing the stark contrasts between various forms of cyberattacks. From the painstakingly slow and calculated infiltrations that demand unwavering discipline and patience, to the fleeting strikes designed to momentarily disrupt the adversary's tactics, Silent Wars scrutinizes the full spectrum of digital offensives.

Venturing into the clandestine strategies of prominent state actors such as the United States, Russia, China, and Iran, Josh's examination of their distinct approaches, strengths, and challenges reveals the complexities of leveraging cyber operations for strategic advantage. Silent Wars unravels the veiled intricacies of this evolving domain, exposing the concealed dynamics that shape the future of covert cyber warfare.

From Calamity To Stability: Harnessing The Wisdom Of Past Financial Crises To Build A Stable And Resilient Global Financial System

In 'From Calamity to Stability: Harnessing the Wisdom of Past Financial Crises to Build a Stable and Resilient Global Financial System', author Josh delves deep into the history of financial crises, examining the causes, impacts, and lessons learned from each event. With a keen analytical approach, Josh expertly navigates the complex landscape of financial regulation, supervision, and policy that has evolved in response to these crises.

Drawing on a wealth of research and firsthand experience, the book presents a comprehensive overview of the regulatory frameworks that have emerged over time, from the Glass-Steagall Act to the Dodd-Frank Wall Street Reform and Consumer Protection Act, as well as the development of international standards such as the Basel Accords. By analyzing the interplay between innovation and stability, Josh identifies key areas where further action is necessary to maintain a resilient financial system capable of supporting sustainable economic growth.

Through a careful examination of the role of international

cooperation, transparency, and trust in fostering financial stability, 'From Calamity to Stability' offers valuable insights into the challenges and opportunities facing policymakers, financial institutions, and society at large. The book not only underscores the importance of learning from past financial crises but also highlights the need for a flexible, forward-looking regulatory framework that can adapt to emerging trends and challenges.

'From Calamity to Stability' is an essential resource for anyone seeking to understand the complex dynamics of the global financial system and the ongoing efforts to ensure its stability and resilience. With its balanced and informed perspective, this book provides a compelling roadmap for navigating the uncertain global economic landscape and building a more secure financial future for all.

The Ultimate Guide To Us Financial Regulations: A Primer For Lawyers And Business Professionals

Over the past several decades, the financial landscape and its regulation have experienced unprecedented growth and transformation. This era has seen significant advancements in financial markets, along with cyclical periods of regulatory reform, often in response to crisis situations. The recent financial crisis has generated immense interest in financial regulation from policymakers, economists, legal practitioners, and academics alike, sparking comprehensive regulatory reforms.
The Ultimate Guide to US Financial Regulations: A Primer for Lawyers and Business Professionals delivers an authoritative, up-to-date, and in-depth examination of the intricacies of financial regulation. With insights on banking, securities, derivatives, insurance, consumer financial protection, anti-money laundering, and international financial regulations, this

comprehensive guide employs a contextual and comparative approach to explore academic, policy, and regulatory requirements.

The initial sections of the guide delve into the foundational themes that underpin financial regulation: financial systems and their regulation; the structure of financial system regulation; the evolution of Financial Regulation; the role of regulatory agencies as well as their various enforcement mechanisms; as well as insurance, banking and securities regulations. The latter sections focus on the core objectives of financial regulation, and explore key topics such as deposit insurance, consumer protection regulations, safety and soundness requirements, insider trading, securities fraud, and investment advisor regulations.

The Ultimate Guide to US Financial Regulations offers an indispensable resource for understanding and navigating the complex world of financial regulation, making it an essential read for professionals across the legal and business spectrum.

Algorithmic Warfare: The Rise Of Autonomous Weapons

Autonomous weapons are changing the face of modern warfare, and their potential impact is both awe-inspiring and unsettling. "Algorithmic Warfare: The Rise of Autonomous Weapons" is a comprehensive analysis of the development, deployment, and ethical considerations of autonomous weapons systems in modern warfare.

By speaking with leading experts in emerging weapons technologies, the author was able to draw in on their firsthand experience and proven expertise to examine the ethical, legal, and strategic implications of these next-generation weapons. From loitering munitions to homing missiles, this book explore how Autonomous Weapons are revolutionizing the battlefield and the way we fight wars.

Through analysis of work written by defense experts, ethicists, and military leaders, this book analyzes the movement to ban autonomous weapons and the legal and ethical issues surrounding their use and spotlights the latest advancements in artificial intelligence in military technology and how they are being used to develop these autonomous systems.

This book also examines the role of national and international regulations and the potential benefits and risks of Autonomous Weapons. With at least 30 countries already developing defensive autonomous weapons that operate under human supervision, it is clear that the ethical questions surrounding this topic grow more pressing each day.

At the forefront of this game-changing debate, "Autonomous Weapons: The Future of Algorithmic Warfare" engages with military history, global policy, and cutting-edge science to argue that we must embrace technology where it can make war more precise and humane, but without surrendering human judgment. When the choice is life or death, there is no replacement for the human heart.

This book is aimed at anyone interested in the future of warfare, from military personnel to policy-makers and concerned citizens alike. From the history of the DOD's Third Offset Strategy to the development of CBRN capable autonomous weapon systems, readers will gain a deep understanding of the current landscape of algorithmic warfare and the challenges and opportunities that lie ahead. It is a must-read for those who want to gain a better understanding of the complex and ever-changing landscape of autonomous weapons and the impact they will have on our world.

Machinery Of War: A Comprehensive Study Of The Post-9/11 Global Arms Trade

In "Machinery of War: A Comprehensive Study of the Post-9/11 Global Arms Trade," Josh offers an exhaustive exploration into the intricate world of global armaments in the aftermath of the tragic events of September 11, 2001. This seminal work probes the depths of the modern arms trade, revealing its multi-faceted nature, its key players, and its profound impact on the geopolitical landscape.

Josh delves into the roles of state actors, private military companies, and non-state entities, underlining their intertwined relationships and the ensuing effects on global security dynamics. With a balanced, objective lens, he navigates through the complexities of cyber warfare, drone technology, and the emergence of autonomous weapons systems, as well as the rise of private military and security companies.

Further, he scrutinizes the arms race in different regions, including the Middle East, Asia, Africa, and Latin America, offering a nuanced understanding of their unique circumstances and their roles in the broader arms trade. The author also addresses the significant role of regulatory efforts in the global arms trade, investigating the successes and failures of arms embargoes and international regulations. Lastly, he gazes into the future, offering predictions and identifying trends that may shape the global arms trade in years to come.

"Machinery of War" is an indispensable resource for policymakers, researchers, scholars, and anyone interested in understanding the complexities of the global arms trade in the 21st century. This in-depth study invites readers to ponder the geopolitical, ethical, and humanitarian implications of the arms trade, highlighting the urgent need for control and regulation in an increasingly interconnected world.

The Insider's Guide To Securities Law: Navigating The Intricacies Of Public And Private Offerings

Navigate the intricate world of private equity and venture capital with "The Insider's Guide to Securities Law: Navigating the Intricacies of Public and Private Offerings." This comprehensive guidebook illuminates the complexities of the industry, serving as an essential resource for legal practitioners, investment professionals, and entrepreneurs alike.

Venture into the fascinating domain of fund formation, understand the roles of limited and general partners, and uncover the strategic aspects of tax structuring. Get acquainted with the key regulatory authorities overseeing the industry, including the Securities and Exchange Commission (SEC), the Financial Industry Regulatory Authority (FINRA), and the Commodity Futures Trading Commission (CFTC).

Delve deeper into the regulatory landscape, exploring crucial compliance requirements, the essentialities of fiduciary duty, and the impact of the JOBS Act and other significant laws. Grasp the essentials of Anti-Money Laundering (AML) and Know Your Customer (KYC) compliance, and learn how to navigate through the processes of sourcing and closing deals, conducting due diligence, and managing and exiting investments effectively.

"The Insider's Guide to Securities Law" offers practical insights, actionable strategies, and a detailed glossary of key terms, making the labyrinth of private equity and venture capital law accessible to both seasoned professionals and newcomers. Embark on a journey through the dynamic landscape of global finance with confidence and insight with this indispensable guide.

The Art Of War In The 21St Century: Timeless Principles For Modern Military Strategy

In "The Art of War in the 21st Century," visionary author Josh brings a fresh perspective to the ancient wisdom of Sun Tzu's renowned treatise. Drawing upon his experience as an entrepreneur and his passion for strategic thinking, Josh explores the timeless principles of "The Art of War" and their applications to modern military strategy.

This book is not a mere translation or interpretation of Sun Tzu's work. Instead, it serves as a bridge between the ancient wisdom of the past and the complex challenges of the present. Josh's unique perspective combines military strategy with insights from the world of business and innovation, offering a fresh take on how these timeless principles can be adapted and applied in the contemporary landscape.

Through engaging narratives, real-world examples, and thought-provoking analysis, Josh demonstrates how Sun Tzu's principles can guide leaders in the 21st century to navigate the complexities of modern warfare. He explores topics such as understanding the operational environment, harnessing technological advancements, fostering effective leadership, and building resilient coalitions.

"The Art of War in the 21st Century" is not solely aimed at military professionals. It is a book for visionary thinkers, entrepreneurs, and leaders from various fields who seek to enhance their strategic acumen and decision-making abilities. It serves as a guidebook for those navigating the ever-evolving landscapes of business, politics, and conflict resolution.

Josh's fresh approach to Sun Tzu's timeless wisdom makes this book an invaluable resource for those seeking innovative strategies to overcome challenges, seize opportunities, and achieve success in the modern world. The author's ability to bridge the gap between ancient principles and contemporary contexts provides readers with practical and thought-provoking insights that transcend traditional boundaries.

Whether you are a military strategist, a business leader, or an aspiring entrepreneur, "The Art of War in the 21st Century" offers a compelling exploration of strategic thinking in our rapidly changing world. Join Josh on this transformative journey and unlock the secrets of Sun Tzu's wisdom, paving the way for strategic brilliance and remarkable achievements in the 21st century.

Silicon And Rare Earth: The Global Contest For Semiconductor And Rare Earth Supremacy

"Silicon and Rare Earth: The Global Contest for Semiconductor and Rare Earth Supremacy" delves into the high-stakes struggle between global powers for dominance in the realms of semiconductors and rare earth elements. As the backbone of modern technology and the driving force behind innovation, these industries have become critical battlegrounds for geopolitical leverage and technological supremacy. In the midst of a global technological cold war, this book offers a comprehensive analysis of the challenges, opportunities, and strategies that nations must navigate to secure their positions in these rapidly evolving markets.

From China's meteoric rise in the semiconductor industry to its strategic monopoly on rare earth elements, this book examines the historical context, environmental impacts, and geopolitical implications of these developments. With an emphasis on the vulnerabilities and risks faced by the United States and the West, it explores the race to secure alternative sources, the importance of international alliances and partnerships, and the role of research and development in fostering innovation and competitiveness.

Drawing on decades of research, 'Silicon and Rare Earth' provides a roadmap for policymakers, industry leaders, and other stakeholders seeking to understand and shape the future of these vital industries. Through a combination of rigorous analysis, case studies, and forward-looking recommendations, this book offers a timely and essential guide to navigating the battle for control in the semiconductor and rare earth industries, amid the broader context of global commerce and international relations in the era of Sino-American decoupling.

Agi And The Thin Blue Line: Unleashing The Power Of Ai In Modern Policing

In an era of rapid technological advancements and unprecedented possibilities, Artificial General Intelligence (AGI) promises to redefine the world of law enforcement. From surveillance and monitoring to predictive policing and proactive crime prevention, AGI has the potential to revolutionize the way police agencies operate and address the complex challenges of public safety. "AGI and the Thin Blue Line: Unleashing the Power of AI in Modern Policing" offers a comprehensive examination of the transformative potential of AGI, its implications, and its practical applications in the field of policing.

This timely book is being released on the verge of the announcement by NYC Mayor Eric Adams that the New York City Police Department is bringing back the Knightscope K5 robots to patrol Times Square alongside with Boston Dynamic's Spot dogs. The fact that autonomous security robots are being used to patrol the streets of New York City, the most populous city in United States, serves as a testament to the rapidly evolving landscape of AI integration in law enforcement.

Structured into seven key chapters, this book investigates the role of AGI in modern law enforcement, showcasing the potential for advanced AI systems to detect and track criminal activities through the analysis of vast data sources. It highlights the applications of AGI in surveillance, pattern recognition, and anomaly detection, while discussing potential challenges in terms of ensuring data security and integrity and it also delves into the ethical and legal implications of AI use in policing, discussing the importance of addressing algorithmic bias, and protecting privacy and civil liberties.

Drawing on insights from professionals, academics, and industry experts, "AGI and the Thin Blue Line: Unleashing the Power of AI in Modern Policing" offers a balanced and forward-looking perspective on the challenges and opportunities presented by AGI in law enforcement. As technology continues to reshape the field of policing, this book serves as a vital resource for policymakers, law enforcement professionals, academics, and anyone interested in understanding the implications and possibilities of AGI in modern policing.

The Quest For Quiet: Cultivating Mindfulness And Solitude In A Noisy World

The Quest for Quiet: Cultivating Mindfulness and Solitude in a Noisy World" is an essential guide for those seeking to find balance, inner peace, and personal growth in the face of the challenges presented by modern society. It is an insightful exploration of the importance of quiet moments for introspection, reflection, and personal growth in today's fast-paced and interconnected society that provides readers with practical guidance on how to create space for solitude and mindfulness in their daily lives, amidst the distractions and demands of modern life.

Drawing on a diverse range of disciplines, including mindfulness practices, meditation techniques, and psychological research, the author, Josh Luberisse discusses the effects of constant connectivity on mental well-being and the ways in which solitude and mindfulness can help individuals navigate the complexities of the contemporary world. Josh addresses the challenges posed by technology and offers practical solutions for reducing screen time, setting boundaries, and cultivating more meaningful connections with ourselves and the world around us.

In "The Quest for Quiet," Josh examines the benefits of mindfulness for personal growth and well-being, highlighting the healing power of spending time in nature, the therapeutic effects of journaling, and the role of minimalism and decluttering in creating a serene environment. He also offers guidance on incorporating mindfulness practices into daily routines and establishing consistent rituals to support personal growth and well-being.

"The Quest for Quiet" is a comprehensive resource for individuals seeking to prioritize solitude and mindfulness in their lives. By providing practical guidance and evidence-based insights, "The Quest for Quiet: Cultivating Mindfulness and Solitude in a Noisy World" empowers readers to embark on a transformative journey towards greater self-awareness, resilience, and appreciation for the simple pleasures of life.

Agi Architects: Building A Symbiotic Civilization With Superintelligent Systems

As artificial general intelligence (AGI) emerges from the realm of science fiction to become a tangible reality, the world stands on the brink of a transformative era. "AI Architects: Building a Symbiotic Civilization with Superintelligent Systems" by Josh explores the potential of AGI-driven systems to revolutionize the way we live, work, and interact in harmony with these powerful technologies.

In this comprehensive and insightful book, Josh delves into the numerous applications of AGI-driven systems, from smart cities and sustainable agriculture to climate change mitigation and space exploration. Central to the discussion is the concept of a symbiotic civilization, where humans and AGI collaborate seamlessly, creating a world that is greater than the sum of its parts.

Josh also addresses the challenges that come with the development and deployment of AGI-driven systems, such as ethical considerations, privacy and surveillance concerns, and governance issues. By offering insights and potential solutions, the book ensures that these technologies are developed and deployed in a manner that aligns with our values and promotes the well-being of all members of society.

As we move toward a future where AGI-driven systems become an integral part of our lives, "AI Architects" explores how we can prepare society for this symbiotic future, fostering the skills and mindset necessary for individuals to thrive in a world where humans and AGI work together.

Join Josh on a journey of discovery, innovation, and collaboration as we explore the potential of AGI-driven systems and their implications for our world. This thought-provoking book will spark curiosity, inspire dialogue, and encourage readers to consider the possibilities and challenges that lie ahead in building a symbiotic civilization with superintelligent systems.

Embracing The Singularity: Envisioning The Future Of Humanity In A World Led By Benevolent Agi

"Embracing the Singularity" is a thought-provoking exploration of a world in which a benevolent Artificial General Intelligence (AGI) has unified humanity and ushered in an era of unparalleled abundance, equality, and harmony. Through a series of interconnected chapters, this compelling work delves deep into the implications of this profound shift, examining its impact on every aspect of human life, from relationships and spirituality to art, culture, and the pursuit of happiness.

Written with a perfect blend of intellectual rigor and heartfelt compassion, this book invites readers to contemplate the challenges and opportunities that lie ahead as we navigate the uncharted territory of a post-Singularity world. By examining the potential of advanced AI to transform our collective and individual evolution, "Embracing the Singularity" provides a comprehensive and nuanced perspective on a future that is both technologically advanced and deeply grounded in empathy, wisdom, and human values.

Throughout its pages, the book fosters a sense of hope and optimism for the future, emphasizing the power of the human spirit and our innate capacity for adaptation, resilience, and growth. With a keen eye for detail and a profound understanding of the complexities of human nature, Josh guides readers on an immersive journey into the heart of a world that is at once familiar and utterly transformed by the Singularity.

"Embracing the Singularity" is an essential read for anyone seeking to understand the implications of advanced AI on our society, as well as those looking to deepen their understanding of the human experience in an age of rapid technological progress. As we stand at the threshold of a new epoch, this book serves as both a roadmap and a source of inspiration, illuminating the path towards a more harmonious, just, and compassionate world.

Join us on this remarkable journey into the unknown, and discover what it truly means to embrace the Singularity.

From Tokenism To Inclusion: A Guide To Diversity, Equity, And Inclusion In The Workplace

"From Tokenism to Inclusion: A Guide to Diversity, Equity, and Inclusion in the Workplace" is a comprehensive and practical guide for businesses and organizations seeking to create a more diverse, equitable, and inclusive workplace. This book offers actionable strategies and best practices for promoting diversity and inclusion, tackling implicit bias, breaking down barriers, and fostering an inclusive culture that empowers all employees.

Drawing on the latest research and real-world examples, this book provides step-by-step guidance on creating and implementing a successful DEI plan, tailored to the specific needs of your organization. From identifying common barriers to creating an inclusive workplace to gaining stakeholder support and measuring progress, this guide covers all aspects of a successful DEI strategy.

Whether you are a small business owner, HR professional, or executive, "Diversity, Equity, and Inclusion: A Practical Guide for Creating a More Equitable Workplace" is a valuable resource for promoting diversity, equity, and inclusion in your workplace. With its clear and concise language, actionable advice, and emphasis on measurable outcomes, this book will help you create a workplace culture that values diversity and fosters inclusion."

Leave No Trace: A Red Teamer's Guide To Zero-Click Exploits

Buckle up and prepare to dive into the thrilling world of Zero-Click Exploits. This isn't your average cybersecurity guide - it's a wild ride through the dark underbelly of the digital world, where zero-click exploits reign supreme.

Join Josh, a seasoned cybersecurity professional and the mastermind behind Greyhat Intelligence & Investigative Solutions, as he spills the beans on these sneaky attacks that can compromise systems without a single click. From Fortune 500 companies to the most guarded government agencies, no one is safe from the lurking dangers of zero-click exploits.

In this witty and engaging book, Josh takes you on a journey that will make your head spin. You'll uncover the secrets behind these stealthy attacks, learning the ins and outs of their mechanics, and unraveling the vulnerabilities they exploit. With real-world examples, he'll keep you on the edge of your seat as you discover the attack vectors, attack surfaces, and the art of social engineering.

But fear not! Josh won't leave you defenseless. He arms you with an arsenal of prevention, mitigation, and defense strategies to fortify your systems against these relentless zero-click invaders. You'll learn how to harden your systems, develop incident response protocols, and become a master of patch management.

But this book isn't all serious business. Josh infuses it with his signature wit and humor, making the complex world of zero-click exploits accessible to anyone with a curious mind and a passion for cybersecurity. So get ready to laugh, learn, and level up your red teaming skills as you navigate this thrilling rollercoaster of a read.

Whether you're a seasoned cybersecurity pro or just starting your journey, "Leave No Trace" is the ultimate guide to understanding, defending against, and maybe even outsmarting the relentless zero-click exploits. It's time to take the fight to the attackers and show them who's boss!

So fasten your seatbelt, grab your favorite energy drink, and get ready to unlock the secrets of zero-click exploits. Your mission, should you choose to accept it, starts now!

The Art Of Network Pivoting And Lateral Movement

"The Art of Network Pivoting and Lateral Movement" is a comprehensive guide for cybersecurity professionals seeking an in-depth understanding of how attackers infiltrate and navigate through networks. Authored by an experienced cybersecurity professional leading a reputable cybersecurity firm, this book serves as a resource for practitioners in the field, focusing specifically on the critical areas of network pivoting and lateral movement.

Throughout the pages, the book explores key tactics, techniques, and procedures employed by cyber attackers, providing valuable insights into their strategies and methods. It delves into practical aspects, including various pivoting techniques such as VPN tunnels, proxy chains, port forwarding, and SOCKS proxies, and lateral movement strategies like credential theft, pass-the-hash attacks, remote code execution, and exploiting software vulnerabilities.

The book also provides an overview of vital tools used in pivoting and lateral movement, along with detailed explanations of how to use them. These range from popular exploitation frameworks like Metasploit and PowerShell Empire to credential harvesting tools like Mimikatz.

More than a technical manual, this book emphasizes the importance of the attacker's mindset in red teaming and encourages ethical hacking practices. It underlines the need to use these skills responsibly, ensuring they contribute to enhancing an organization's security posture rather than undermining it.

"The Art of Network Pivoting and Lateral Movement" is a must-have for any cybersecurity professional's library. Whether you're a red teamer aiming to refine your skills, a blue teamer looking to understand the strategies employed by attackers, or a cybersecurity enthusiast eager to learn more, this book provides a well-rounded, detailed perspective on network pivoting and lateral movement in cybersecurity.

From Prey To Predator: An Evolutionary Tale Of Hunting, Warfare, And Human Survival

"From Prey to Predator: An Evolutionary Tale of Hunting, Warfare, and Human Survival" is a riveting journey through time that marries anthropology, history, and survival science in a fresh and engaging way. Discover how the human species transformed from vulnerable prey into dominant predators, and explore the striking parallels between hunting and warfare as survival strategies.

This captivating narrative unveils the vital role of preparedness in human survival, demonstrating why hope alone is not a survival strategy. Drawing on the rich tapestry of our ancestral past, this book explores the timeless cycle of life and death, revealing how our place within this cycle has shaped our strategies for survival.

Perfect for history enthusiasts, survivalists, and anyone interested in human evolution, this book presents a thought-provoking examination of humanity's instinct for survival. Discover why physical fitness and mental toughness were – and remain – crucial for survival, and how community, adaptability, and innovation have played their parts in our survival story.

"From Prey to Predator" takes you on a thrilling journey from our humble origins to our place in the modern world, exploring how lessons from our past can guide our future. As we navigate the complexities of the 21st century, this book serves as a timely reminder of the resilience, ingenuity, and survival instinct that pulses through our veins. Dive into this intriguing exploration of human survival and uncover the story of humanity's relentless drive to survive and thrive.

The Art Of Exploit Development: A Practical Guide To Writing Custom Exploits For Red Teamers

In an era where cyber threats loom large, understanding the art of exploit development is essential for any cybersecurity professional. This book is an invaluable guide for those looking to gain a deep understanding of this critical aspect of cybersecurity.

"The Art of Exploit Development: A Practical Guide to Writing Custom Exploits for Red Teamers" delivers an exhaustive, hands-on tour through the entire exploit development process. Crafted by an experienced cybersecurity professional, this resource is not just a theoretical exploration, but a practical guide rooted in real-world applications. It balances technical depth with accessible language, ensuring it's equally beneficial for newcomers and seasoned professionals.

The book begins with a comprehensive exploration of vulnerability discovery, guiding readers through the various types of vulnerabilities, the tools and techniques for discovering them, and the strategies for testing and validating potential vulnerabilities. From there, it dives deep into the core principles of exploit development, including an exploration of memory management, stack and heap overflows, format string vulnerabilities, and more.

But this guide doesn't stop at the fundamentals. It extends into more advanced areas, discussing how to write shellcode for different platforms and architectures, obfuscate and encode shellcode, bypass modern defensive measures, and exploit vulnerabilities on various platforms. It also provides a thorough look at the use of exploit development tools and frameworks, along with a structured approach to exploit development.

"The Art of Exploit Development" also recognizes the importance of responsible cybersecurity practices. It delves into the ethical considerations of exploit development, outlines secure coding practices, runtime exploit prevention techniques, and discusses effective security testing and penetration testing.

Complete with an extensive glossary and appendices that include reference material, case studies, and further learning resources, this book is a complete package, providing a comprehensive understanding of exploit development.

With "The Art of Exploit Development," you're not just reading a book—you're enhancing your toolkit, advancing your skillset, and evolving your understanding of one of the most vital aspects of cybersecurity today.

The Ethical Hacker's Handbook: A Comprehensive Guide To Cybersecurity Assessment

Get ready to venture into the world of ethical hacking with your trusty guide, Josh, in this comprehensive and enlightening book, "The Ethical Hacker's Handbook: A Comprehensive Guide to Cybersecurity Assessment". Josh isn't just your typical cybersecurity guru; he's the charismatic and experienced CEO of a successful penetration testing company, and he's here to make your journey into the fascinating realm of cybersecurity as engaging as it is educational.

Dive into the deep end of ethical hacking as Josh de-mystifies complex concepts and navigates you through the murky waters of cyber threats. He'll show you how the pros get things done, equipping you with the skills to understand and test the security of networks, systems, and applications - all without drowning in unnecessary jargon.

Whether you're a complete novice or a seasoned professional, this book is filled with sage advice, practical exercises, and genuine insider knowledge that will propel you on your journey. From breaking down the complexities of Kali Linux, to mastering the art of the spear-phishing technique, to getting intimate with the OWASP Top Ten, Josh is with you every step of the way.

Don't expect a dull textbook read, though! Josh keeps things light with witty anecdotes and real-world examples that keep the pages turning. You'll not only learn the ropes of ethical hacking, you'll understand why each knot is tied the way it is.

By the time you turn the last page of this guide, you'll be

prepared to tackle the ever-evolving landscape of cybersecurity. You might not have started this journey as an ethical hacker, but with "The Ethical Hacker's Handbook: A Comprehensive Guide to Cybersecurity Assessment", you'll definitely finish as one. So, ready to dive in and surf the cyber waves with Josh? Your journey to becoming an ethical hacking pro awaits!

Eyes In The Sky: A Global Perspective On The Role Of Uavs In Intelligence, Surveillance, Reconnaissance, And Security

From the simple plaything of hobbyists to the high-tech guardians of national security, the story of Unmanned Aerial Vehicles (UAVs) is a thrilling flight into the frontier of technological innovation. "Eyes in the Sky" charts this breathtaking ascent, offering readers an inside look at the machines and systems shaping the modern world, both in the air and on the ground.

Embark on a journey that spans continents, delving deep into the extraordinary uses of UAVs across military, civilian, and commercial sectors. Learn how these devices gather intelligence, conduct surveillance, and even wage war. Explore how, far from the battlefield, they monitor traffic, patrol borders, and aid humanitarian efforts.

But, like Icarus soaring too close to the sun, the story of UAVs isn't without its darker shades. In an age of cyber threats and geopolitical tension, the skies aren't always friendly. Witness how these mechanical marvels are used by criminals, terrorists, and cyber pirates, exploiting their strengths for nefarious purposes.

This comprehensive examination of UAVs wouldn't be complete without an exploration of what's being done to keep us safe. Through countermeasures and cybersecurity, witness the ongoing struggle between those who exploit technology and those who safeguard it.

From cutting-edge counter-drone technologies to the ethical hackers combating these airborne threats, this narrative unravels the complex world of UAVs, their implications for global security, and the measures in place to maintain the balance.

"Eyes in the Sky" is not just a tale of technology—it's a chronicle of change, detailing how we've reshaped the heavens to serve our needs. With unparalleled access to the latest trends and greatest minds in the field, this book is a must-read for technophiles, security enthusiasts, and anyone curious about our rapidly evolving world.

Fasten your seatbelts, dear readers. It's time to take off into a sky full of drones!

Who Decides What's True?: Navigating Misinformation And Free Speech In The Social Media Landscape

In the rapidly evolving digital age, the pursuit of truth has become a high-stakes game of hide-and-seek. As misinformation and disinformation percolate through the vast networks of social media, the line between fact and fiction seems increasingly blurred. At the heart of this tumultuous landscape is a paradox: Social media platforms, designed to facilitate free expression and global connectivity, have become both the guardians of information and the gateways to a labyrinth of falsehoods.

"Who Decides What's True?" is a deep dive into these complex, interconnected issues. In this book, Josh demystifies the nature of truth in the digital age, probes the anatomy of misinformation, and wrestles with the moral, ethical, and legal challenges of content moderation.

Chapter by chapter, Josh unpacks the evolution of social media from mere communication tools to the de facto public squares of discourse. He delves into the reach and influence of these platforms, revealing the double-edged sword they wield in disseminating both knowledge and falsehoods. Through comprehensive analyses, he confronts the implications of misinformation, from political manipulation and election interference to public health crises and social unrest.

At its core, the book grapples with a critical dilemma: How can freedom of speech be preserved on platforms inundated with harmful misinformation? This question forms the axis around which the exploration of content moderation revolves. Examining the role and responsibilities of social media platforms, the book sheds light on the operational and ethical challenges they face in the curation of content. It also scrutinizes the vital role of fact-checking organizations and the mechanisms for independent oversight of content decisions.

The narrative then ventures into possible strategies for navigating this murky terrain. From fostering media literacy and critical thinking to implementing platform features and tools for combating misinformation, the book presents potential pathways towards a more truthful digital world.

In its final sections, "Who Decides What's True?" takes a bold stride into the future, anticipating potential regulatory changes and their implications for social media. It dissects the intersecting concerns of data privacy and user rights, all while speculating about the impact of emerging technologies on the propagation of misinformation.

Anchored in extensive research and informed analysis, this book is a necessary read for anyone looking to understand the complexities of truth, freedom of speech, and social media in today's interconnected world. It provides a blueprint for navigating the vast, often confusing terrain of digital discourse. It asks the tough questions, challenges assumptions, and invites its readers to participate in a crucial conversation about the role of truth in the age of social media. This book is more than just a critical exploration; it's a call to action for everyone who believes in the value of truth and the power of informed dialogue.

Made in the USA
Middletown, DE
06 September 2024